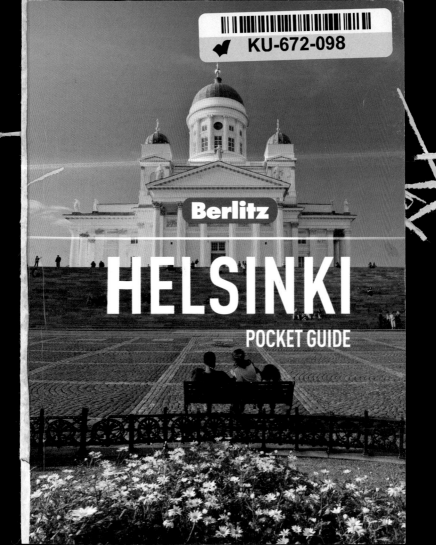

Berlitz

HELSINKI

POCKET GUIDE

KU-672-098

Walking Eye
mobile app

Discover the world's best destinations with the Insight Guides Walking Eye app, available to download for free in the App Store and Google Play.

The container app provides easy access to fantastic free content on events and activities taking place in your current location or chosen destination, with the possibility of booking, as well as the regularly-updated Insight Guides travel blog: Inspire Me. In addition, you can purchase curated, premium destination guides through the app, which feature local highlights, hotel, bar, restaurant and shopping listings, an A to Z of practical information and more. Or purchase and download Insight Guides eBooks straight to your device.

TOP 10 ATTRACTIONS

SUOMENLINNA FORTRESS
A Unesco World Heritage site, guarding the Gulf of Finland. See page 60.

SENATE SQUARE
Pristine 19th-century town planning. See page 34.

ESPLANADI
This long, elegant park is lined with Finland's flagship design stores. See page 29.

TEMPPELIAUKIO
The Rock Church is hewn from solid stone and shrouded in shining copper. See page 44.

MARKET SQUARE AND HALL
Buy bear meat, wild strawberries or fish direct from bobbing boats. See page 30.

NATIONAL MUSEUM OF FINLAND
Explore Finland's history from the Stone Age to the present day. See page 43.

KIASMA
This striking gallery challenges visitors with its avant-garde exhibitions. See page 40.

USPENSKI ORTHODOX CATHEDRAL
The red-brick edifice proclaims Russia's might from its hilltop in Katajanokka district. See page 33.

KAMPPI CHAPEL OF SILENCE
A hallowed space by the bustling bus station. See page 39.

ATENEUM ART MUSEUM
The Ateneum contains the largest collection of art in Finland. See page 28.

A PERFECT DAY

9.00am

Helsinki Cathedral

After feasting on a Finnish breakfast at your hotel, head straight for the neoclassical Kruununhaka district. In the morning light, before the crowds descend, the startling white cathedral floats above Senate Square like a dream.

10.00am

Havis Amanda

Wander down Unioninkatu to have a gander at the city's sauciest mermaid. Next, stop at the orange tents on the Market Square for a fortifying slug of coffee before admiring the many stalls, tumbling with fresh produce.

1.00pm

Lunch in Esplanadi Park

Back on dry land, head for lunch at the 140-year-old Restaurant Kappeli (see page 111), in prime position on tree-lined Eteläesplanadi. A favourite of Sibelius's, the restaurant has one of the biggest terraces in the city, perfect for people-watching and listening to live music on the nearby summer stage.

11.00am

Archipelago tour

Helsinki is a city of the sea. The Royal Line boat tour threads between the archipelago islands, offering stunning views of Suomenlinna Fortress and a whole new perspective on the city.

2.00pm

Walk up Mannerheimintie

Stroll through the park to the beginning of Mannerheimintie. This is Helsinki's longest street: on the left-hand side are venerable institutions such as the Parliament Building and the National Museum; while on the right are the modern Kiasma and Musikkitalo. Stop at Finlandia Hall to admire the work of Alvar Aalto, one of Finland's greatest architects, before taking a pleasant walk across Hesperia Park to the Olympic Stadium.

IN HELSINKI

5.00pm

Sauna

Catch tram No. 8 (Arabia direction) along Helsinginkatu, and prepare yourself for a quintessentially Finnish experience. Kotiharjun, dating back to 1928, is a rustic wood-burning sauna where you can get to know the locals. Pace yourself with plenty of breaks and cold water. If you're here on Tuesday, Friday or Saturday, be brave and get a scrub from the traditional washing-woman.

8.00pm

Death metal?

Helsinki's operas and orchestras take a well-deserved rest over the summer, but the city is full of music. Bar Bäkkäri is a rock/metal bar with a fantastic atmosphere; if that's not to your liking, you're guaranteed a good time at the Happy Jazz Club Storyville, with live music every night in summer.

4.00pm

Olympic Stadium Tower

Although the Olympics were held here over 60 years ago, walking into the stadium will still give you goosebumps. However, the highlight of a visit is a clanking lift ride up the tower for fabulous views of Helsinki and its archipelago backdrop.

6.30pm

Sámi dining

The metro from Sörnäinen will whisk you back to the centre in 10 minutes, hopefully with an appetite. Lappi Ravintola (see page 114), a cosy wooden affair on Annankatu, can supply a taste of the wild north, with dishes of reindeer, wild mushroom, and Lappish cheese served with cloudberry jam.

CONTENTS

INTRODUCTION

If you're looking for riotous razzamatazz, a sleepless, strung-out, 24-hour city where the party never ends, look elsewhere. Helsinki is a city of cool northern charms, floating serenely above the hot-headed European mainland. One of the world's newest capitals, it is a city that rewards the curious. If you want something unusual – fascinating architecture and design, off-beat galleries and museums, a piquant blending of east and west – you've come to the right place.

Helsinki is one of the world's most liveable cities, a safe, tolerant, modern metropolis with a clear identity. Startling new buildings are transforming the city's silhouette, but its dwellers are still people of the forests and lakes at heart, with a passion for nature that is reflected in Helsinki's many gorgeous parks and gardens.

CITY OF THE SEA

Long referred to as the "Daughter of the Baltic", Helsinki owes its fortune to the sea. The city was founded to compete with the Hanseatic port of Tallinn, just across the Gulf of Finland, and the great offshore fortress Suomenlinna was built 200 years later to protect this vital harbour. In post-war years, shipbuilding was a major industry, and Helsinki is still a centre for specialised Arctic ships, with 60 percent of the world's icebreakers being built in its western dockyards. Today, however, cruise ships have taken over from the merchant vessels and battleships, bringing in 400,000 visitors each summer.

The sea and Helsinki are intrinsically linked. Salty inlets poke their way into metropolitan boulevards, and countless yachts and ferries thread their way through the archipelago islands. The city has even captured a piece of the Baltic and built a kind of shrine around its edges. Public edifices such as Musikkitalo Music Centre, the Winter Gardens, the brand-new library, Linnanmäki amusement park, and two stand-out Alvar Aalto buildings, the Opera House and Finlandia Hall, encircle Töölönlahti Bay, the peaceful watery core of the city's cultural and recreational area. The entire Katajanokka district, stuffed with Art Nouveau buildings, appears to be tethered to the mainland,

Café life

floating alongside it like a boat. Fishermen still sail their catches into the harbour, mooring beside the bustling Market Square to sell their wares. And as if Helsinki doesn't have enough saltwater, a brand-new lido is currently being constructed nearby, underneath the spinning shadow of the SkyWheel.

Only during the long, cold winter does the water finally rest. Even the Baltic freezes into an endless expanse on which promenaders can walk dogs or try out their cross-country skis. At the weekend, city-dwellers strap on their skates and take an icy spin around the inlying islands of the archipelago.

MEET THE FINNS

In Helsinki, 83.2 percent of the people are Finnish-speaking and 6.0 percent Swedish-speaking. Notwithstanding the overwhelming dominance of Finnish, the city's street signs are more often than not shown in both languages – with Swedish beneath the Finnish.

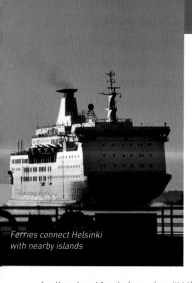

Ferries connect Helsinki with nearby islands

Whatever their language, the Finns, by and large, are quiet people and to outsiders may seem rather introspective. But make an overture and you'll receive real kindness and curiosity in return.

Finns are patriotic – their national flag is on display everywhere – and are rightly proud of their country's natural beauty. A great deal of importance is placed on spending time in the whispering forests of spruce and birch. In high summer, city-dwellers head for their rustic *mökki* (summer cabin) on the shores of a glassy lake. Escaping into nature is vital to the Finnish soul. Helsinki's offshore islands are popular beach and bathing places in summer, and there are two national parks on its doorstep to go fishing, or picking berries and mushrooms as autumn draws in.

Conversely, Finns also have a rampant addiction to technology – perhaps not so surprising, since Finland is the home of Nokia. The City of Helsinki has opened up data to its citizens, so that everyone can participate in improving its public services, and much of the centre is covered by its free Wi-Fi network.

ARCHITECTURAL HERITAGE

Helsinki was founded in 1550, and only evolved into a large city in the late 19th century. Consequently, it has not grown up from higgledy-piggledy medieval roots like most other European cities, but had an orderly plan from the start. After it was made Finland's capital in 1812, Helsinki benefited from the astonishing talents of German architect Carl Ludwig Engel, who poured his creativity into Senate Square and its surroundings. Another wave of fine architecture arrived with the nationalist movement in the 20th century, when Jugendstil (the German version of Art Nouveau) and then Finnish Functionalism transformed the cityscape once more.

The city's fine architectural past gives it the confidence to create inspired present-day works. Helsinki was the World Design Capital in 2012, with €16 million spent on innovative projects, including the Kamppi Chapel of Silence and the Kulttuurisauna public sauna.

Helsinki also has big dreams for the future: its run-down industrial areas and former docklands are being rejuvenated. The old abattoir quarter is now a centre for food; Suvilahti power plant is a dramatic new venue for open-air music festivals; and Kalasatama harbour is turning into a visionary residential area, with eco-designed high rises and floating apartments, due to open in 2030.

CULTURE

Finns are culture vultures: this small capital has no fewer than 80 museums, many of which, such as the Ateneum National Gallery and the contemporary Kiasma, are focused on art and design.

⊙ CLASSICAL MUSIC

This country of just 5.5 million has also produced a disproportionate number of conductors and classical performers. The importance that Helsinki gives to its musicians is reflected in the prominence of buildings such as Finlandia Hall, Musikkitalo and the Opera House, which sit in stately splendour alongside the Parliament and National Museum. Finnish composer Jean Sibelius (1865–1957) is celebrated in frequent concerts.

A BRIEF HISTORY

Finland is one of Europe's newer countries: it celebrated its 100th birthday in 2017. However, this vast, sprawling territory has been the stamping ground of many different peoples across the centuries. The first definitive evidence of human settlement shows that Sámi people had moved into the region by around 8300 BC. The Sámi were gradually displaced into the far north by incoming Fenno-Ugrian tribes, who migrated from the Ural Mountains and the Volga River plains, located to the southeast in present-day Russia. By 2000–1000 BC, forms of Finnish were spoken on both sides of the Gulf of Finland.

The early settlers were subsistence hunters and fishermen, but by around 500 BC, agriculture had become the dominant way of life. Stable settlements grew up first along Finland's coast, spreading inland by the middle of the Finnish Iron Age. Around AD 800–1050, Vikings occupied what is now the southern coast-line of Finland as a trade route to the east.

THE SWEDISH ERA

During the early Medieval period, the area now known as Finland was coveted by both its western and eastern neighbours – the Roman Catholic Swedes and the Greek Orthodox Novgorod Republic (Russia). Sweden mounted three Crusades against Russia, with the territory of Karelia being the juicy fought-over bone. The Third Crusade, in 1293, split Karelia between east and west, establishing the Catholic–Orthodox border that was to stand for many centuries. Vyborg/Viipuri, with its imposing castle, was founded to defend the line.

Swedish political and social systems flourished, but Finnish peasants retained their personal freedom and were never serfs.

Finns were given the right to vote in the election for the king in 1362 and later for representation in the Swedish Diet (parliament). From the late 14th to the early 16th century Denmark, Norway and Sweden were united in the Kalmar Union. The Lutheran Reformation reached Finland in 1527, initiating a surge of interest in the Finnish language. The prominent proponent of the Reformation, Mikael Agricola (1510–57), Bishop of

A 16th-century map of the Nordic countries and Lapland

Turku and creator of written Finnish, translated the New Testament into that language in 1548.

THE FOUNDING OF HELSINKI

Helsinki, or Helsingfors in Swedish, was founded by King Gustav Vasa of Sweden to offer trading competition to Tallinn, the Hanseatic League city on the opposite side of the Gulf of Finland. To achieve this he issued an edict, on 12 June 1550, ordering citizens from Rauma, Ulvila, Tammisaari and Porvoo to move into the new town at the mouth of the River Vantaa. This date is now celebrated as Helsinki Day. At that time the town was very small, and became even smaller when many of its inhabitants were killed by plague and a great fire that struck in 1570. Growth was slow, but continuing wars saw Helsinki become an important military centre and a winter haven for the navy. By 1640 the town had moved to its present location, further south on the Vironniemi headland.

In 1654 another great fire caused devastation, only to be followed in 1710 by a further outbreak of plague that killed approximately 1,200 people – around two-thirds of the population.

In 1700 the Great Northern War broke out between Sweden and Russia, and in 1703, Russia, a growing power, built a new capital at nearby St Petersburg. During what was known as the 'Great Hate', from 1713–21, Russia occupied Helsinki. The Russians were driven out, returned two decades later; and after this, Sweden's position as a superpower began to wane. The Swedes reinforced Helsinki against the Russian threat by beginning construction, in 1748, of the sea-fortress of Sveaborg – now Suomenlinna – on a series of small islands guarding the marine approaches to the city (see page 60). When completed some 40 years later, it was considered the 'Gibraltar of the North'.

The Battle of Poltava ended Swedish domination

This brought increased prosperity to Helsinki, and seafaring trade developed significantly, but more trouble was on the horizon. Fires destroyed Helsinki in 1808 and, in the same year, political machinations between Napoleon and Tsar Alexander I forced Sweden into the disastrous decision of declaring war on Russia. In the Peace Treaty signed the following year, the Swedes

> ### Ode to the brave
>
> Finland's national poet, Johan Ludvig Runeberg (1804-77), wrote the epic poem *The Tales of Ensign Stål*, which commemorates the bravery of the Finns during the disastrous 1808-09 war. The first section of the poem was later adopted as Finland's national anthem, *Vårt land (Our Land)*.

accepted that they had lost control of Finland. The country was then annexed to Russia as an Autonomous Grand Duchy in 1809.

RUSSIAN RULE

Finland's new ruler, the Russian Emperor Alexander I (1809–25), proved lenient. Finland was given an extensive amount of autonomy, and was able to retain both its Lutheran religion and Swedish as the official language. In 1812, Helsinki replaced Turku as the capital of the Grand Duchy of Finland. In 1827 Finland's only university burned down in the Great Fire of Turku; when it reopened the following year, it did so in Helsinki.

Helsinki flourished under Russian rule, with the new capital rebuilt in monumental Empire style by Carl Ludwig Engel and Johan Albrecht Ehrenström. During this period the city's population increased to around 50,000 – four decades earlier it had been just 4,000 – and daily life was very similar to that in other European cities. Kaivopuisto and Hanko Spas were extremely popular with the affluent classes, who were

The South Harbour in 1895

not allowed, by law, to travel outside the empire to seek such pleasures elsewhere.

This period of peace and prosperity ended with the Crimean War (1853–56), which was fought on many fronts. Sveaborg (Suomenlinna), the gateway to St Petersburg, was bombarded by 20,000 shells during a period of 46 hours, but remained standing.

FINNISH VERSUS SWEDISH

During the reign of Alexander II (1855–81) sections of the population began agitating for the Finnish language to be a joint official language with Swedish, an end achieved in 1866. After more than 50 years of absence, the Finnish Diet met in 1863, and 15 years later the Conscription Act raised a Finnish army.

Helsinki became Finland's administrative centre, and the opening of railway lines – to Hämeenlinna in 1862 and St Petersburg in 1870 – ensured that it also became the industrial heart of the country. Coinciding with this industrialisation, grand neo-Renaissance buildings – most notably along Esplanadi, Aleksanterinkatu, Mannerheimintie and Erottaja – began gracing the city. Finally, after a period of more than 300 years, Helsinki achieved the primary ambition of King Gustav Vasa of Sweden, and eclipsed Tallinn as the most important city on the Gulf of Finland.

As Russian nationalism flourished during the reign of Alexander III (1881–94), and even more so during that of Nicolas II (1894–1917), its adherents grew impatient with the privileges

THE FATHER OF FINLAND

Carl Gustaf Emil Mannerheim (1867–1951) is one of Finland's greatest heroes, a warrior who pitted his country's meagre forces against the might of Russia in three bitter wars. He was perhaps an unlikely figurehead: Mannerheim served in the Russian Imperial Army for 30 years. However, following the October Revolution, his allegiance was all to Finland.

Mannerheim's most memorable leadership came during the Winter War of 1939–40. Appointed Commander-in-Chief of the Finnish forces, he oversaw a guerrilla offensive against Russia that lasted a brutal 105 days. The Red Army had vastly superior numbers, but the Finns were fast, adaptable and equipped to deal with temperatures that fell as low as –43°C. Russian casualties were almost five times higher than those of the Finns, causing great embarrassment to the Russian regime.

After World War II, Mannerheim became president of Finland, guiding the country from war to peace. Such was his prestige that his funeral, on a bitter winter day in 1951, brought Helsinki to a standstill. The Mannerheim Museum (see page 55) is a fascinating memorial to the Father of Finland.

enjoyed by the autonomous Grand Duchy of Finland. Russification, the policy of overturning Finnish separatism, flourished in Russia, although Finland itself was undergoing radical reform. The old Swedish Diet was replaced by a unicameral parliament in 1906, with MPs voted for by universal suffrage. Finland was the first country in Europe, and second in the world (after New Zealand), to allow women to vote and to stand as MPs, and its first parliamentary session had a total of 19 women representatives.

INDEPENDENCE

The new century saw the construction in Helsinki of grand new buildings like the Central Railway Station, the National Museum and Kallio Church, all in Art Nouveau (*Jugendstil*) style. The first Finnish opera was performed in 1852, and this became an established national art form. Jean Sibelius (1865–1957), composer of nationalistic works such as the *Karelia Suite* (1893) and *Finlandia* (1899), was awarded a lifetime state grant in 1897 so that he could concentrate on composition.

As Russia underwent the October Revolution, Finland seized the opportunity to declare independence on 6 December 1917, and Helsinki became the capital of the Sovereign Republic of Finland. Yet the ongoing presence of Russian troops within the new country's boundaries caused turmoil that resulted in a bloody civil war. A coalition of Finnish Socialists and the Russian Red Guard was pitted against General Carl Gustav Emil Mannerheim's White Army,

International settlers

Over the last 10 years, the number of foreigners living in Helsinki has more than doubled. Today, foreign-language residents make up 14 per cent of Helsinki's population, with the largest groups coming from Russia, Estonia and Somalia.

backed by the Imperial German Army. Following the Russian defeat, Finland's independence was assured. After flirting with the idea of becoming a monarchy, Finland adopted a republican constitution in 1919.

Shortly afterwards a new style of architecture surfaced, most notably in the silhouette of the parliament building (1931), and the stadium built for the 1940 Olympics (postponed until 1952 by the outbreak of war).

Mannerheim

On 30 November 1939, over a million troops from the Soviet Union attacked Finland. The Finns, heavily outnumbered, repulsed the attacks and inflicted heavy losses on the Russians, but were forced to cede the southeastern part of the country.

During the so-called Continuation War (1941–44) Helsinki was attacked by much heavier air raids but suffered comparatively little damage; Finland was the only country in continental Europe involved in World War II not to be occupied by foreign forces.

THE YEARS OF DANGER

During the period 1944–48, known as the Years of Danger, a communist takeover was still a possibility. This threat was averted by the Treaty of Friendship, Co-operation and Mutual Assistance (known as YYA in Finland) with the Soviet Union in 1948. This guaranteed Finland's sovereignty, but committed the country to defend its borders against Germany, or any state aligned with Germany,

Alvar Aalto's Finlandia Hall

that could use Finland to attack the Soviet Union.

The post-war years saw Finland struggling to pay off immense war reparations to the USSR. The government invested heavily in the metal and ship-building industries, and Finland changed rapidly from a mainly agrarian to a modern industrial country. The debt was finally paid in 1952, after which the country began to look outwards once more. Finland joined the United Nations in 1955, and became a full member of the European Union in 1995. With its growing confidence, a new, more modern, style of architecture emerged, epitomised by the work of Alvar Aalto: examples in Helsinki include Finlandia Hall (1971) and the Opera House (1993).

MODERN HELSINKI

Today, Helsinki has a population of almost 630,000, a figure which is expected to increase by 45,000 by 2030. To deal with this, there are ambitious projects to transform the former harbour/industrial areas Jätkäsaari and Kalasatama into new commercial and residential areas, and to extend the metro system. The centre too is changing: new homes are being built along the western side of the railway lines, and there are ambitious plans for the Töölönlahti Bay area (see page 45). The urban structure of Helsinki is altering more rapidly than at any time during the past hundred years.

HISTORICAL LANDMARKS

c. 10,000 BC First inhabitants arrive in Finland as the glaciers retreat.

500 BC–AD 1300 Finnish Iron Age.

1155-1293 Three Swedish Crusades against Russia.

1527 Lutheran Reformation reaches Sweden.

12 June 1550 King Gustav Vasa of Sweden founds Helsinki.

1713–21 and 1742 Russia occupies Helsinki, marking Sweden's decline as a superpower.

1748 Construction of Suomenlinna fortress begins.

1808-09 Sweden declares war on Russia and is defeated; Finland annexed to Russia as an Autonomous Grand Duchy.

1812 Helsinki becomes the capital city, and is rebuilt in monumental Empire style.

1866 Finnish made the joint official language with Swedish.

1906 Finland introduces universal suffrage, becoming the first European country to grant women the vote.

6 December 1917 Finland takes advantage of the Russian October Revolution to declare independence: a short civil war follows.

1919 Finland adopts a republican constitution.

30 November 1939 The Soviet Union attacks, but is repulsed by Finland's vastly inferior number of troops.

post-war years Finland evolves from an agrarian country to an industrial one.

1952 Helsinki hosts the XV Olympic Games, postponed from 1940 by World War II.

1955 Finland becomes a member of the United Nations.

1970s onwards Alvar Aalto initiates a modern style of architecture.

1 January 1995 Finland joins the European Union.

2000 450th anniversary of the city; Helsinki is European City of Culture.

2002 The euro replaces the Finnish mark.

2013 Finland's flagship company Nokia is sold to Microsoft.

2015 The city celebrates the 150th anniversary of Sibelius's birth.

6 December 2017 Finland celebrates 100 years of independence.

Tram passing by an Art Nouveau building

WHERE TO GO

Helsinki is on an oddly shaped peninsula, nibbled at by the Gulf of Finland, which convolutes itself into numerous inlets, bays and harbours around the edges of the city. Initially, this can be a little disorientating; but you'll soon find your way around. This is a small capital, and most of its attractions are centrally located. Before striking out independently, it can be worthwhile taking the **Panorama Sightseeing Bus Tour** (see page 125), which gives a good overview of the city's main sights with a recorded commentary in multiple languages.

Visitors arriving by train or airport bus will be deposited at the Central Railway Station, at the very core of the city. The station sits in the northwest corner of a rectangular area between Mannerheimintie to the west, the Esplanadi in the south, and the Senate Square and Market Hall to the southeast. It is within this rectangle that the majority of Helsinki's hotels, shops, bars and nightclubs are to be found.

Cruise ships dock at one of four harbours: South Harbour, Katajanokka (both around 1.5km/1 mile southeast of the station), West Harbour and Hernesaari (both around 3.5km/2.2 miles southwest of the station). All are linked to the centre by frequent trams or buses.

Most places of interest can be reached comfortably on foot, but if you are footsore or short of time, there's a good public transport network. This includes a metro (subway) system, although most visitors prefer to remain above ground and use the tram or bus systems, which all converge at Central Railway Station.

It's hardly worth hiring a car, even if you're exploring further afield. There are frequent train services to Tampere and Turku, both just under two hours away; and Porvoo can be reached by

Wikström's solemn figures adorn Helsinki Railway Station

a short bus ride. Tallinn, in Estonia, on the south side of the Bay of Finland, is linked to Helsinki by high-speed ferry.

RAUTATIENTORI

The **Central Railway Station ❶** (Päärautatieasema) is Finland's most-visited building: more than 200,000 people pass through it each day. Designed by Eliel Saarinen and inaugurated in 1919, it links two of Helsinki's most prevalent architectural styles, National Romanticism and Functionalism. The monumental structure certainly makes a strong first impression on visitors: sheer pink-granite walls make ants of the hurrying crowds, and the massive, four-sided clock tower is a prominent landmark. The station's front doors are guarded by four muscular giants, the *Lyktbärarna*, each holding a translucent lantern. These solemn figures, designed by Emil

Wikström, were taken down for a bath in 2013 – a complicated task when even a single head weighs 1.5 tonnes. Commuter and long-distance trains, including trains to Russia, leave from the Central Railway Stations, and the central Metro station lies below it.

Railway Station Square (Rautatientori), to the east of the building, serves as an open-air bus station and has, on its north side, the National-Romantic-style Finnish National Theatre, which has been the theatrical company's home since 1902. An oversized statue of playwright and novelist Alexis Kivi (1834–72) stands outside. He is now recognised as one of Finland's greatest writers, although he died in obscurity.

⦿ WINTER IN HELSINKI

The nights may be long and the weather bitter, but so what! As the Finns say, "Life gets no better by pulling a face"; and there are plenty of attractions to stave off the winter darkness.

The twinkling fairy lights of St. Thomas Christmas Market fill Senate Square for most of December; the night sky explodes with fireworks on New Year's Eve; and in early January, the Lux Helsinki light festival makes the city glow – literally.

And of course this is the time for seasonal ice-and-snow fun. The whole of the Railway Square is transformed into an open-air ice-skating rink, IcePark (tel: 040 775; http://ice park.fi; Mon–Fri 2–9pm, Sat–Sun 10am–9pm; charge), while Keskuspuisto (Central Park), just north of the Olympic Stadium, contains 180km (112 miles) of cross-country skiing trails.

When the skies are cold and clear, you can also see the Northern Lights from Helsinki – pick a dark corner of the city and watch for the pulsing, flickering light show.

ATENEUM ART MUSEUM

On the south side of Rautatientori, at Kaivokatu 2, is the neo-classical façade of the **Ateneum Art Museum, The National Gallery of Finland** ❷ (Ateneumin Taidemuseo, Suomen Kansallisgalleria; tel: 0294 500 401; www.ateneum.fi; Tue and Fri 10am–6pm, Wed–Thur 10am–8pm, Sat–Sun 10am–5pm; charge). Inaugurated in 1887, it represented a huge investment for a small country, and its collection of more than 20,000 works of art is the largest in Finland. The works of Finnish artists date from the 1750s to the early 1960s (works from 1960 onwards are on display at the Kiasma, Museum of Contemporary Art, see page 40). Much-loved national treasures include Akseli Gallen-Kallela's *Boy with a Crow* (1884) and two pieces inspired by Finnish mythology, *Lemminkäinen's Mother* (1897) and the *Aino Myth* triptych (1891); Hugo Simbert's enigmatic *The Garden of Death* (1896) and *The Wounded Angel* (1903); and several beautiful works by Albert Edelfelt depicting scenes of rural Finnish life. There's also a small selection of international art (Van Gogh, Gauguin, Cézanne and Chagall).

Stockmann's department store ❸ (see page 95) a Helsinki institution, takes up an entire city block at the junction with Mannerheimintie. The stand-out sculpture here

The National Gallery of Finland is housed in the 19th-century Ateneum is the **Three Smiths statue** (1932) by Felix Nylund, depicting three naked blacksmiths hammering on an anvil. If you look carefully around the base, you can still see damage caused by bomb shrapnel, inflicted during the 1944 Continuation War.

THE ESPLANADI

The elegant semicircular façade of the **Swedish Theatre** (Svenska Teatern), dating from 1866, dominates the

western end of the **Esplanadi ❹**, Helsinki's most emblematic park. Two streets – Pohjoisesplanadi (North Esplanade) and Eteläesplanadi (South Esplanade) – run either side of the long, narrow strip of greenery, all the way down to Market Square. Pohjoisesplanadi is home to small shops, bars and restaurants, including the ever-popular Café Esplanad, the Kämp Hotel, and the tourist office (No. 19), while Eteläesplanadi has larger institutions. These two elegant neo-Renaissance rows replaced older wooden buildings in the second half of the 19th century.

The bronze figure in the middle of the park is J. L. Runeberg (1804–77), the national poet who wrote the lyrics for the Finnish national anthem. Two other statues of eminent men at the western end commemorate the writer Zacharias Topelius (1818–98), and the poet Eino Leino (1878–1926). At the eastern end of the park is the city's most famous statue, *Havis Amanda* ❺. Erected in 1908, the fountain features a naked mermaid intended to represent Helsinki rising from the sea. It

The Old Market Hall overlooks the South Harbour

was unveiled amid great controversy, but today is one of most widely admired symbols of the city. At 6pm on Walpurgis Night (30th April), students gather to wash the statue and place a tasselled cap on her head, marking the start of the carnivalesque May Day celebrations.

MARKET AND SENATE SQUARES

The bustling **Market Square ⑥** (Kauppatori) is one of Helsinki's real delights. Its year-round market (Mon–Fri 6.30am–6pm, Sat 6.30am–4pm, summer also Sun 10am–5pm) bursts with colourful produce and souvenirs in summer, and you can buy fresh fish directly from small boats moored at the quayside. If you're peckish, there's also a motley collection of outdoor cafés housed in tents. The square is the venue for the lively Baltic Herring Market, a week-long seafood festival held each

October. It quietens down during winter, but is still worth a visit. The granite **obelisk** topped by a two-headed eagle was Helsinki's first public memorial, erected in 1835 to commemorate Empress Alexandra's visit to the city two years before. The eagle was removed by Russian sailors during the Revolution, but flew back to its golden perch in 1971.

Along Eteläranta, the now renovated red-, white- and yellow-brick **Old Market Hall** ❼ (http://vanhakauppahalli.fi; Mon–Sat 8am–6pm, Sun 10am–5pm) offers a fascinating array of stalls selling delicatessen-style foods, including bear meat, bakery products and all kinds of other goodies.

Massive Tallink Silja ferries dock in the **South Harbour** opposite. In winter, the frozen sea can reach a thickness of 50cm (20in) – an impressive fleet of icebreakers keeps the channels clear. Ferry boats to Suomenlinna (see page 60) depart from this harbour. Between May and September, you can also catch a boat here for an archipelago cruise. Three companies offer 1.5-hour Helsinki sightseeing trips: **IHA-Lines** (tel: 09 6874 5050; www.ihalines.fi), **Strömma Finland** (tel: 092 288 1600; www.stromma.fi) and **Royal Line** (tel: 0207 118 333; www.royalline.fi). The latter also have cruises to destinations a little further afield, such as to Porvoo or to its offshore Söder-skär lighthouse.

Across the street from the Market Square, the long, low building with the bluish-grey façade is the **City Hall** (Pohjoisesplanadi 11–13), dating from 1896, with the city's coat-of-arms depicted on the tympanum. The stately white building on the corner is the **Presidential Palace**, constructed in 1820 by a merchant with grand ideas. Seventeen years later, it was purchased by the Russian Tsar to serve as his local palace when visiting Finland. After Finland gained independence, the building became the official residence of the president. The building is still used for important presidential receptions, but these days the man himself lives in a more modern house near Seurasaari.

On cobbled Sofiankatu, **Helsinki City Museum** ❽ (Helsingin kaupunginmuseo; tel: 09 3103 6630; www.helsinginkaupungin museo.fi; Mon–Fri 11am–7pm, Sat–Sun 11am–5pm; free) has frequently changing exhibitions that always unveil some interesting aspect of Helsinki's history.

KATAJANOKKA DISTRICT

Katajanokka, a boomerang-shaped island jutting from the eastern side of the city, is connected to the centre by two short bridges where locals like to cast their fishing rods. The district contains a ferry port and a quiet, well-to-do residential area, whose elegant streets make for pleasant wandering.

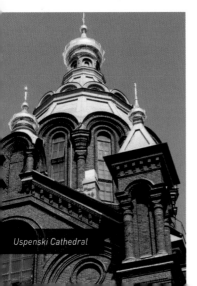
Uspenski Cathedral

Unfortunately, the first thing you see crossing the Kanavakatu Bridge on to Katajanokka is one of Alvar Aalto's least successful efforts: the dirty white marble Enso Gutzeit Office Building (the "sugar cube"), dated 1962.

Helsinki Allas (tel: 04 0565 6582 www.helsinki allas.fi; Mon–Fri 6.15am–11pm, Sat–Sun 8am–11pm; charge) is an exciting new harbourside development located between the Market Square and the beginning of Katajanokka. It consists of a spa, saunas, two full-length sea-water swimming pools, a children's pool and a diving pool. On the quayside next to the site, the 40-metre (130ft-) high **FINNAIR SkyWheel** (tel: 040 480 4604; www.skywheel.fi; Mon–Fri 10am–9pm, Sat 10am–10pm, Sun 11am–7pm; charge) takes you on a 12-minute revolution, with views of the Market Square and the city's two cathedrals.

Uspenski Cathedral ❾ (Tue–Fri 9.30am–4pm, Sat 10am–3pm, Sun noon–3pm; May–Sept also Mon 9.30am–4pm; closed Orthodox feast days; free), consecrated in 1868, is the district's most captivating sight. This brick behemoth is the largest Orthodox cathedral in the Western world, built to make a statement after the Russians defeated the Swedes in 1809. Its green copper roof is studded with 13 small golden cupolas, representing Christ and the Apostles – it's actually more impressive from the inside, where four immense painted granite columns support the star-studded dome. Glittering chandeliers and a gilded iconostasis add to the air of opulence.

A further 100m/yards from the cathedral is **Luotsikatu** ❿, Helsinki's best-preserved street of Art Nouveau (*Jugendstil*) houses. Many of the buildings on this and nearby streets were designed by the architectural team of Gesellius, Lindgren and Saarinen, and all abound with unusual details. Don't miss the beautiful carved door at No. 1 or the sad-looking little creatures above the entrance at No. 5.

Other interesting structures on the island include the ice-breakers moored on the northern side; the long, yellow 19th-century naval barracks (Merikasarmi), designed by Engel, which now house the Finnish Foreign Ministry; Helsinki's former county prison (Helsingin lääninvankila), transformed in 2007 into a rather unusual hotel; and the *Jugendstil* Customs and Bonded Warehouse (1900), beside the Viking Line terminal, with its grey turrets and round red-brick towers.

Cathedral and statue of
Alexander II on Senate Square

SENATE SQUARE

The historical **Kruununhaka** district contains many fine 19th-century buildings. After Sweden's defeat in 1809, Helsinki became the capital city of the newly-created Grand Duchy of Finland. Tsar Alexander I naturally wanted a capital worthy of the name. He chose Johan Albrecht Ehrenström, a military engineer, to sweep away the cramped medieval streets and put something splendid in their place. In Ehrenström's vision, **Senate Square** **⓫** (Senaatintori) would become the symbolic heart of the new Grand Duchy, with all the main institutions placed around it according to a strict hierarchy of function. The Prussian architect Carl Ludvig Engel (1778–1840) was chosen to design and oversee the whole project, a job that took him a quarter of a century and resulted in some 30 dazzling neoclassical buildings.

Today the square is a national meeting place; huge, excited crowds gather for celebrations such as Independence Day, 6

December, and New Year's Eve. A statue of the "good Tsar" Alexander II watches over the festivities from the centre of the square. Dating from 1894, the statue is surrounded by images representing Law (*Lex*), Peace (*Pax*), Light (*Lux*) and Work (*Labour*). Stand at the Tsar's feet to best hear the sound installation **Senaatintorin Ääni**, a five-minute digital carillon composed by Harri Viitanen and Jyrki Alakuijala, which plays at 5.49pm every day.

HELSINKI CATHEDRAL

The shining white **Helsinki Cathedral** (Tuomiokirkko; tel: 09 2340 6120; daily 9am–6pm, until midnight in summer; free) dominates Senate Square, its massive columned façade topped by a huge dome. The building is in the shape of a Greek cruciform and is sparsely decorated, inside and out. From the rooftop, 3m- (9.8ft-) tall statues of the Apostles gaze over the city, the largest collection of zinc sculptures in the world. The only focus points in the curving white interior are the gilded organ, pulpit and altarpiece, flanked by angels, and statues of the Reformation leaders Luther, Melanchton and Mikael Agricola.

Engel worked on the cathedral blueprints from 1818 until his death in 1840. Construction began during his lifetime, but it was not until 15 February 1852 that the building was consecrated. It was originally known as the Church of St Nicholas – after both the patron saint of trade and

Guard Parade

The Guard Parade has become a popular sight in the city. At 12.30pm on summer Fridays, the Finnish Defence Force band marches with much pomp and ceremony from Senate Square to Esplanadi Park, where an hour-long concert then takes place.

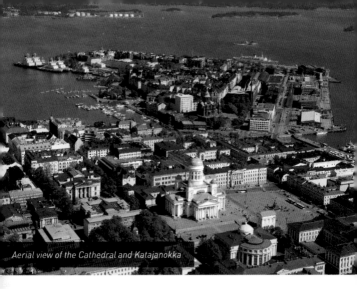
Aerial view of the Cathedral and Katajanokka

seafaring, and Tsar Nicholas I – and was upgraded to cathedral status in 1959.

The cathedral can seat a congregation of 1,300, and the vaulted crypt is used as a venue for exhibitions and concerts. Engel also designed the two chapels on either side of the two-tiered bank of steep steps; the one to the east is still used as a chapel, and the bells and a café are contained in the western one.

STATE BUILDINGS AND THE UNIVERSITY

The first building to be constructed on Senate Square was the eastern Imperial Senate (1822), which became known as the **Palace of the Council of State** after Finnish independence. Today it houses the prime minister's office, the office of the chancellor of justice, much of the ministry of finance, and the government's conference rooms – cabinet meetings are held here every Thursday at 1pm. The columns and porticoes of the pastel-coloured building were designed to reflect the Roman Senate. The country's oldest public clock, the handiwork of master clockmaker Jaako Juhonpoika Könni, adorns the façade.

Turku Academy, the country's first university, was founded in Turku in 1640 but was destroyed by a devastating fire in 1828. Turku's sad loss was Helsinki's gain: the university was transferred to the young capital and given a prestigious location on the west side of the Senate Square. It was renamed the Tsar Alexander University, and renamed again in 1919 to become the **University of Helsinki**.

Adjacent to the cathedral, the pale-yellow Empire-style **University Library** (tel: 02941 23920; www.helsinki.fi/kirjasto; Mon–Fri 9am–8pm, Sat 10am–4pm; free) is one of the world's most beautiful library buildings and is considered Engel's masterpiece. Take a few minutes to admire the marvellously ornate Cupola Hall, designed to resemble Roman baths. The upper area is supported by 28 marble columns, their pinnacles gilded with gold leaf, with the images and ornaments on the domed ceiling symbolising knowledge and learning. Unfortunately, Engel didn't live long enough to witness the library's opening in 1840.

Behind the square, on Aleksanterinkatu 16–18, and recognisable by its blue

Palace of the Council of State

façade and white columns, is **Sederholm House** (Sederholmin Talo; tel: 09 3103 6529), which dates from 1757 and is the oldest stone building in Helsinki. It belongs to the city council, and now houses the Helsinki City Museum, a favourite with the little ones with its fun Children's Town.

MANNERHEIMINTIE

Mannerheimintie, Helsinki's busiest and longest street, was named after the respected Marshal of Finland in honour of his 75th birthday in 1942. Baron Carl Gustav Emil Mannerheim (1867–1951) was a political and military leader, explorer, general in the Russian Imperial Army and President of Finland from 1944–46, and perhaps the most influential figure in Finnish

⊙ THE FOUR ESTATES

Before the present parliamentary system came into being, the country was governed by a Four-Estate Diet. The votes of three of the four Estates (Nobility, Clergy, Burghers and Peasants) were required to carry through a parliamentary decision. Sitting beside a little park to the east of Senate Square is the House of Nobility (Ritarihuone), a brick building with Gothic influences that dates from 1862. This house was built as a meeting place for the Noble Estate, and members of the Finnish aristocracy still occupy it today.

The three non-noble Estates had to share premises: the **House of Estates** (1890), behind the cathedral on Snellmaninkatu, was their meeting place. The frieze on the tympanum depicts Emperor Alexander I surrounded by the heads of the Four Estates and the symbols of faith and justice.

history from the Civil War to the late 1940s. Helsinki has a museum dedicated to his memory (see page 55).

Majestic buildings line either side of the street – mainly modern on one side and traditional on the other – with many of Finland's major political and cultural institutions, such as its Parliament and the National Museum, among them.

The internationally acclaimed Kamppi Chapel of Silence

KAMPPI

Just off the southern end of Mannerheimintie is **Kamppi**, a busy shopping and travel centre, containing two underground bus stations and a Metro station. Take a moment away from the rushing crowds and step into another of Helsinki's one-of-a-kind churches. The award-winning **Kamppi Chapel of Silence** (tel: 09-2340 2018; Mon–Fri 8am–8pm, Sat–Sun 10am–6pm) is an astonishing building, constructed from curving strips of spruce.

Over the road, on Yrjönkatu, is the **Amos Anderson Art Museum** ⑬ (tel: 684 4460; www.amosanderson.fi; Mon, Thur and Fri 10am–6pm, Wed until 8pm, Sat–Sun 11am–5pm; charge), the biggest private art collection in Finland. It is housed in the impressive 1913 home and offices of Amos Anderson (1878–1961), a businessman and philanthropist who owned several printing houses and *Hufvudstadsbladet* – the country's largest Swedish-language newspaper. He was an avid collector of 20th-century Finnish art, and the works he amassed are on display.

There are also 8 to 12 temporary exhibitions held here every year.

Once you've looked round the museum, treat yourself to a cocktail and a panoramic view of the city from the **Ateljee Bar**, on the 14th floor of Sokos Torni Hotel next door.

Two 1930s Functionalist buildings can be found close to Kamppi. **Lasipalatsi** ("Glass Palace"), on Mannerheimintie, has been rejuvenated to create a welcoming media centre with an internet library; and **Tennispalatsi** ("Tennis Palace"), used for basketball matches during the 1952 Olympic Games, now houses Finland's largest cinema complex and the **Helsinki City Art Museum** ⑭ (Helsingin Taidemuseo Tennispalatsi; tel: 09-310 1051; www.helsingintaidemuseo.fi; Tue–Sun 11am–7pm). The museum hosts interesting temporary exhibitions and has a section dedicated to Tove Jansson, of Moomins fame.

MANNERHEIMINTIE'S SIGHTS

Kiasma ⑮ (Kiasma, Nykytaiteen museo; Mannerheiminaukio 2, tel: 0294 500 501; www.kiasma.fi; Tues 10am–5pm, Wed–Fri 10am–8.30pm, Sat 10am–6pm, Sun 10am–5pm; charge, but free first Friday of month and for under-18s), the city's museum of contemporary art, is found in an amazing asymmetrical 1990s building, created by American architect Steven Holl and since completely renovated. The structure was designed to maximise the amount of light entering the building, and its oddly

Urban design

Those interested in town planning, architecture and urban design might like to pop into Laituri (tel: 09-310 37390; http://laituri.hel.fi; Mon–Thur 10am–7pm, Fri until 4pm, Sat noon–4pm; free), where the City of Helsinki's Planning Department has exhibitions showing off its exciting redevelopment plans.

Kiasma, Helsinki's reigning museum of contemporary art

shaped windows also afford views of key landmarks. Its bold exhibitions of avant-garde Finnish and international contemporary art change three times per year. Outside, an impressive **equestrian statue** of Marshal Mannerheim is especially striking when illuminated at night.

At No. 30, the stately **Finnish Parliament Building** ⑯, with its 14 Corinthian columns and a wide set of steps, was constructed in 1931 from the finest red Finnish granite. Arguably the best-known building in Finland, this is where the 200 members of the Eduskunta, the Finnish legislature, meet. When in session, proceedings can be viewed from the public gallery. There is also a **visitor centre** (Arkadiankatu 3, Mon–Fri 10am–4pm), in an annex around the corner from the main building.

Opposite Parliament is the music centre **Musiikkitalo** ⑰ (tel: 020 707 0400; www.musiikkitalo.fi), the home of the Helsinki Philharmonic Orchestra, the Finnish Radio Symphony

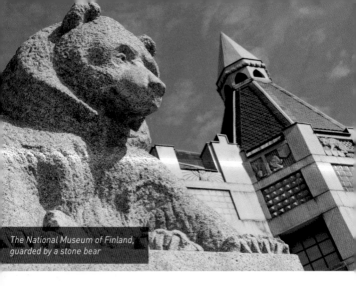
The National Museum of Finland, guarded by a stone bear

Orchestra and the Sibelius Academy. Its understated architecture is deliberate – it was designed to blend in rather than compete with its prestigious neighbours. The acoustics of its six concert halls, however, are second to none – Japanese acoustician Yasuhisa Toyota created each one to host a specific kind of music, from early music to electronica. A new square, **Kansalaistori**, setting for the Taste of Helsinki food festival (see page 99), was also created to link the new building with Kiasma.

The attractive pink **Hakasalmi Villa** ⑱ (tel: 09 3107 8519; http://hakasalmivilla.fi; Tue–Wed, Fri–Sun 11am–5pm, Thur 11am–7pm) sits unobtrusively in a pleasant English garden set back from the road. It was built in 1846 and was once the home of a wealthy benefactor, Aurora Karamzin, who died here in 1902. Today it is a branch of the City Museum, holding changing art, history and folklore exhibitions throughout the year.

The eye-catching façade and tower of the **National Museum of Finland** ⑲ (Suomen kansallismuseo; tel: 295 33 6000; www.nba.fi/en/nationalmuseum; Tues–Sun 11am–6pm; charge, but free Fri 4–6pm), built in National Romantic style to resemble a medieval church or castle, dates from the early 1900s. Its huge metal bears are guarded by a stone bear, an important national symbol, while inside the entrance hall ceiling is decorated with scenes from the Kalevala, painted by Akseli Gallen-Kallela. The exhibits themselves detail the development of Finnish life from the prehistoric era to present times, and are divided into six departments: "Prehistory of Finland" is the country's largest permanent archaeological exhibition; "Treasure Troves" is a sparkling collection of coins, medals, decorations, silver and weapons; "Realm – Swedish rule" and "Realm – Swedish and Russian rule" detail Finnish culture and society from the Middle Ages to the 19th century; "A Land and its People" documents life before industrialisation; and "Suomi Finland" investigates daily 20th-century living. The collection of the former **Museum of Cultures**, documenting different peoples of the world, is also found here. On the third floor is an interactive exhibition for children (see page 98).

NATURAL HISTORY MUSEUM AND TEMPPELIAUKIO CHURCH

A large bronze elk (made by one of the museum's taxidermists) hints at the contents of the distinguished neo-baroque building standing 300m (328 yards) along Arkadiankatu. The **Finnish Museum of Natural History** ⑳ (Luomus; tel: 02941 28800; winter Tues–Sun 10am–5pm, Thur until 6pm June–Aug, Tues–Fri 9am–4pm, Thur until 8pm, Sat 10am–5pm, Sun 10am–4pm Sept–May; charge; www.luomus.fi) contains a small but interesting collection of bones and some vivid taxidermy dioramas. Pick up a free headset for English explanations.

Temppeliaukion church is built into the rock

Kunsthalle Helsinki ㉑ (tel: 040 450 7211; Tues, Thur, Fri 11am–6pm, Wed 11am–8pm, Sat–Sun 11am–5pm; charge; http://taidehalli.fi) has no collections of its own, but hosts six to eight major contemporary art exhibitions, curated from studios, galleries and museums elsewhere, every year. Retrospectives of esteemed Finnish (Eero Saarinen, Alvar Aalto) and international (Arne Jacobsen, Helmut Newton, Andy Warhol, Anish Kapoor) figures have been held here; the hall also promotes the work of up-and-coming artists.

Continue a further 300m/yards northwest to find one of Helsinki's most famous tourist attractions. The **Rock Church** ㉒ (Temppeliaukion kirkko; tel: 09 2340 6320; check tel. 09 2340 5940 for opening hours; www.helsinginkirkot.fi) is an architectural oddity, quarried out of solid bedrock. The inner stone walls are topped by a massive copper dome with a diameter of 24m (79ft). It is lined with 22km (13 miles) of copper stripping, and light is reflected inwards from 180 skylights. It can hold a congregation of nearly one thousand and is a popular concert venue due to its excellent acoustics. Designed by the architect brothers Timo and Tuomo Suomalainen, the church was hugely controversial when it opened in 1969, but now attracts up to 8,000 visitors a day in summer. It's a good idea to come first or last thing in the day to avoid the worst crowding.

TÖÖLÖNLAHTI BAY AND THE OLYMPIC STADIUM

Töölönlahti Bay is a wonderful thing to see in a capital city. Black-headed gulls hover like hummingbirds over its glinting waters before diving for fish, and a popular walking path runs through the surrounding Hesperia Park.

⊙ CITY PLANNING, HELSINKI STYLE

In the 1950s, an ambitious development plan, overseen by Alvar Aalto, was made to transform Töölönlahti Bay and the strip of land directly to its south into a utopian cultural and recreational area, lined with landmark public buildings. In the event, Finlandia Hall (1971) was the only structure to appear, at the southern end of the lake. However, 20 years later, the City of Helsinki resurrected the idea of a turning the bay into a "living room" for its citizens. Finlandia Hall was joined by the Opera House (1993), Kiasma (1998) and Musikkitalo (2011). In 2016, the striking timber-clad Löyly public sauna and restaurant was the trigger for the regeneration of the industrial Hernesaari harbourside.

And new in 2018 is the much-anticipated Helsinki Central Library (http://keskustakirjasto.fi), located close to Musikkitalo. An international competition was launched in 2012 to choose a design, with the winning proposal "Käännös" selected in 2014. Designed by ALA Architects, the three-storey building is a dreamy creation of glass and twisted Siberian larch timbers that looks as though it is floating in air. The building contains a library, event areas and, this being Finland, a public sauna.

The plan was always for the bay to form the centre of a large cultural area. Directly by the waterside is the modernist **Finlandia Hall** ㉓ (tel: 09 40 241; www.finlandiatalo.fi; closed except for guided tours and events; information shop open Mon–Fri 9am–5pm), one of Finland's most iconic buildings. This masterpiece was designed, right down to the doorknobs, by renowned Finnish architect Alvar Aalto in 1962. However, since its completion in 1971, bitter Finnish winters have warped the Carraran marble used to create its striking white exterior, and leaps in acoustic technology have seen the Musiikkitalo (2011) take over as the country's pre-eminent venue for classical music. Today Finlandiatalo is mainly used as a unique and highly impressive conference centre, but there are plans afoot to make it more accessible to the public with pedestrian walkways and a terraced café overlooking the bay.

Café overlooking the bay and Finlandia Hall

Next to the hall is the small **Hakasalmi Park**, whose main feature is a stainless-steel pool that is illuminated from below. The four bronze hands on top of high posts behind the pool are a monument to Urho Kekkonen, President of Finland from 1956 to 1981, whose name is engraved in a rock behind the pool. The president was known for often using his hands to express himself, and even wrote exclusively by hand rather than with a typewriter.

At the end of the park is another impressive modern structure – considered Finnish architecture at its finest. Regular opera performances were held in Finland for 120 years before the **Finnish National Opera** ㉔ (Helsinginkatu 58; tel: 09 4030 2211; www.operafin.fi) moved to its new home here in 1993. There are performances of opera, ballet or classical music six nights a week – original-language performances are surtitled in Finnish, Swedish and English.

Beyond the northern end of Töölönlahti Bay, the **City Winter Garden** (Hammarskjöldintie 1, tel: 09 3103 9985; Tues 9am–3pm, Wed–Fri noon–3pm, Sat–Sun 12–4pm; free) is a particularly peaceful haven. Established in 1893 it consists of a small formal garden with statuary, with pheasants running around, and a large, decorative greenhouse featuring an attractive combination of exotic plants, a fish pond and various pieces of modern art. The rose garden opens daily from 7am to 9pm in summer.

The most dominant structure by far is the 72m (236ft) tower of the **Olympic Stadium** ㉕ (tel: 09-436 6010; www.stadion.fi; closed for renovation until 2019, check the website for reopening date and times), and a visit to the two-level caged-in observation platform is recommended. The views are, quite simply, the finest in Helsinki and offer a panoramic perspective of the city and its surrounding archipelago.

Finland's excellent results in the Olympics of the 1920s led to dreams of holding the games in Helsinki. The city bid to be the 1940 host country, and the stadium, deemed to be one of the most beautiful in the world, was inaugurated on 2 June 1938. However, the Games were postponed due to World War II, and Helsinki did not get to host them until 1952. The stadium set its capacity record of 70,435 people during the competition; today it is still in use, pulling in up to 40,000 people for international sporting and musical events.

Also within the stadium complex is the **Sports Museum of Finland** (Urheilumuseo; tel: 09-434 2250; www.urheilumuseo. fi; also closed until 2019, check website for reopening date and times). It has 30,000 multimedia exhibits and more than 200,000 photographs depicting great moments – both of victory and defeat – in the history of Finnish athletics. In front of the stadium a nude **statue of Paavo Nurmi** (1897–1973) celebrates one of the greatest of all Finnish athletes.

The **Sibelius Monument** 26 (1967) is a much-visited memorial dedicated to the revered Finnish composer, Jean Sibelius.

⊙ THE FLYING FINN

Sisu is a quality that the Finns pride: it conjures up toughness, independence, and grisly determination in the face of adversity. Paavo Nurmi (1897–1973), a middle- and long-distance runner, was the personification of *sisu*. A multiple world record-breaker, Nurmi won nine Olympic gold medals and three silvers in his 12 Olympic races, and is still remembered today for his extraordinary running style, speed and tough character.

Nurmi had running in his blood from an early age. Although his father, a religious man, disapproved of such a frivolous pastime, Nurmi exerted his independence and spent every spare moment running with boys in his neighbourhood and alone in the woods. At a time when the fledgling Finnish republic was struggling to build a cohesive identity, Nurmi came to be its sporting ambassador, winning worldwide admiration and acclaim as the Flying Finn.

Created by Eila Hiltunen, it consists of over 600 welded steel tubes and weighs a whopping 24 tonnes. It is located in the pleasant Sibelius Park in the northwestern Taka-Töölö district.

THE "DESIGN DISTRICT"

When Helsinki became World Design Capital in 2012, the city invested heavily in promoting Finnish design. The "Design District" is an area of 25 streets south of the Central Railway Station, containing almost 200 designer boutiques, studios, galleries and museums. It centres around the Design Museum and the Museum of Finnish Architecture, and touches four districts, Kaartinkaupunki, Kamppi, Punavuori and Ullanlinna. A map of the Design District is available from the tourist office. Even if you aren't in the mood for shopping, there are plenty of interesting sights to see in this bohemian area.

ART AND ARCHITECTURE

The **Design Museum** ㉗ (Designmuseo; tel: 09 622 0540; www.designmuseo.fi; June–Aug daily 11am–6pm; Sept–May Tues 11am–8pm, Wed–Sun 11am–6pm; charge) focuses on industrial art and design and artistic handicrafts, with a permanent collection of more than 75,000 design objects, from the second half of the 19th century to the present. If you love Alvar Aalto, Kaj Franck, Oiva Toikka, Eero Saarinen, Tapio Wirkkala and others of their ilk, this is the place to see their work close-up.

Just behind the museum, at Kasarmikatu 24, is the moderately interesting **Museum of Finnish Architecture** (Suomen Rakennustaiteen museo; tel: 8567 5100; www.mfa.fi; Tues, Thur–Sun 11am–6pm, Wed 11am–8pm; charge) in a neo-Renaissance building that was originally constructed for the Learned Societies in 1899.

Diagonally opposite is the neo-Gothic silhouette of **St John's Church** ㉘ (Johanneksen kirkko; Korkeavuorenkatu 12; tel: 09 2340 7730; www.helsinginkirkot.fi; summer Mon–Fri 10am–3pm, Sun for mass), the largest church in Helsinki, with its two piercing stiletto spires. Towards the end of the 19th century the growing population of Helsinki rendered the cathedral and the Old Church inadequate, and this third Lutheran place of worship was built. It has excellent acoustics and is a particular favourite for choral concerts.

Another impressive building is the **Mikael Agricola Church** ㉙ (1935) (tel: 09 2340 6123), designed by Lars Sonck in a mix of Art Nouveau and classical styles and easily identified by its hypodermic-like 30m (98 ft) spire. The spike can be retracted into the tower using a series of pulleys: this was done in World War II to confuse Russian bombers. Architecture fans might like to continue down Tehtaankatu, turning right into **Huvilakatu**, which contains some of the most attractive Art Nouveau houses in the city.

BULEVARDI AND HIETALAHTI MARKET

Beginning where Esplanadi stops, **Bulevardi** is an impressive street containing beautiful late 19th- and early 20th-century buildings. Near its northeastern end you'll find Helsinki's oldest church, called, appropriately enough, the **Old Church** 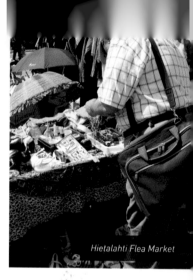 (Vanha kirkko; Lönnrotinkatu 6; tel: 09 2340 6128; Mon–Wed and Fri noon–3pm, Thur noon–8.30pm). The

Hietalahti Flea Market

church is Engel-designed, but was only supposed to be a temporary structure until the new cathedral was ready. It was thrown together in 1826 using planks of wood, and was never given any bells. However, by the time the cathedral was consecrated 26 years later, the city's population had increased so much that the Old Church was retained as a permanent place of worship. The church sits in a beautiful if macabre park: two-thirds of Helsinki's population were buried here in 1710, following an outbreak of plague.

Further down the street, in its own cobbled block, is the elegant **Alexander Theatre** (tel: 09 676 980; www.aleksanterin teatteri.fi). Named after Tsar Alexander II, it was built voluntarily by Russian officer engineers and conscripted soldiers, and staged its first performance in 1879. Today it is the site of many concerts, musicals and stage performances, mostly in Finnish.

Cable Factory

The Sinebrychoff brewery, dating from 1819, once sat at the end of Bulevardi. It relocated in the early 1990s, but its name is preserved in the **Sinebrychoff Art Museum** ❸❶ (Sinebrychoffin taidemuseo; tel: 09 1733 6460; Tue, Thur and Fri 11am–6pm, Wed 10am–8pm, Sat–Sun 10am–5pm; charge; www.sinebrychoff intaidemuseo.fi). This three-storey, Empire-style house was donated to the state by Paul and Fanny Sinebrychoff in 1921, along with its collections of Old Flemish, Dutch, Italian and French paintings, Swedish portraits, Russian icons, silver, china and antique furniture.

Directly across the road, **Hietalahti Market Hall** ❸❷ (www.hietalahdenkauppahalli.fi; Mon–Thur 8am–6pm, Fri–Sat 8am–10pm, Sun 8am–5pm) is an Art Nouveau structure, with an enticing array of produce on its 116 stalls. Outside, in summer, you will find just about everything up to, and including, the kitchen sink at **Hietalahti Flea Market** (https://hiet sunkirppis.fi; Mon–Fri 8am–6pm, Sat 8am–4pm, summer also Sun 10am–4pm).

ALONG THE WATERSIDE

The **Cable Factory** ❸❸ (Tallberginkatu 1; tel: 09 4763 8330; www.kaapelitehdas.fi) cultural centre is located in converted

U-shaped warehouses, out on the west of Helsinki. Nokia's former stamping ground houses an array of cultural facilities, including three esoteric museums, 12 galleries, and numerous art and music studios. Most people come here for specific shows and festivals: take a look at the website for upcoming events. Take the Metro to the Ruoholahti stop, from where the centre is an 800m/yards walk.

ULLANLINNA AND KAIVOPUISTO

South of Market Square are two well-heeled districts, Ullanlinna and Kaivopuisto, composed of pretty parkland, stately embassies and beautiful old homes.

OBSERVATORY HILL

Tähtitorninmäki – which literally means "star-tower hill" – is an attractive park that rises above the northeastern end of Ullanlinna, allowing for views over the South Harbour. At the top you'll find an astronomy exhibition inside **Helsinki Observatory** ㉞ (tel: 02 941 24244; Fri–Sun noon–4pm, Thur noon-8pm; www.observatorio.fi), another Engeö-designed building whose revolving observation tower tested the architect's ingenuity.

Around the base of the hill, the formidable **Russian Embassy & Consulate** commands a whole block, and was built in 1952 as part of Finland's war reparations to the Soviet Union. Opposite is the **Cathedral of St Henry** (Pyhän Henrikin Katedraali; Pyhän Henrikin aukio 1; tel: 09 637 853; http://henrik. katolinen.fi), built in neo-Gothic style. One of Helsinki's two Catholic churches, it was originally opened in 1860 as a garrison church. Nearby is Robert Stigell's bronze memorial, the **Statue of the Shipwrecked**, a well-known landmark.

KAIVOPUISTO PARK

Helsinki's favourite green space is **Kaivopuisto Park** ㉟. In summer, the city sponsors free concerts here, and Kaivopuisto overflows with happy locals, sunbathing, picnicking, strolling, and admiring the fine views across to Suomenlinna.

It's hard to believe that the park was a wasteland until the 1830s. At this time, Russians were forbidden to travel outside the empire, so for relaxation the upper classes were taken by steamer to enjoy the delights of Helsinki, St Petersburg and Tallinn. High-flying businessman Henrik Borgström cashed in on the situation by developing the cosmopolitan Kaivohuone spa on the headland. However the Crimean War in the 1850s, and the subsequent lifting of the ban on foreign travel, soon

Kaivopuisto Park

brought this ritzy era to an end. The former spa, dating from 1838, now houses a restaurant.

The most ornate of the Empire-era **villas** sits on the corner of Kalliolinnantie and Itäinen Puistotie. It dates from 1839 and is the oldest preserved building in the park.

At Kalliolinnantie 8, the delightful wooden villa with the octagonal tower houses the **Cygnaeus Gallery** ❸ (tel: 09 4050 9628; daily 11am–5pm; charge), the oldest art museum in Finland. Its main exhibition consists of a 19th-century collection of Finnish art donated to the country by poet and critic Fredrik Cygnaeus (1807–81), professor of aesthetics and literature at Helsinki University.

Nearby, the more formidable building at Kalliolinnantie 14 belonged to one of Finland's most enigmatic and revered men, the Marshal of Finland Baron Carl Gustav Mannerheim (see page 19). The fascinating **Mannerheim Museum** ❸ (tel: 09 635 443; www.mannerheim-museo.fi; Fri–Sun 11am–4pm; charge) is housed in the 1870s Borman Villa, where Mannerheim once lived. Opened in 1951, and preserved as it was at Mannerheim's death, the exhibits include uniforms, medals and other personal memorabilia, as well as his extensive East Asian collections. The engaging guides do a great job of bringing his complex character to life.

SEA VIEWS

The highest point in the park is the tiny **Ursa Observatory**, from where there are fabulous panoramic views (in winter, the observatory hill is also Helsinki's prime sledging spot!).

At the end of the park, **Café Ursula** (tel: 09 652 817; Mon–Tue 9am–9pm, Wed–Sat 9am–10pm, Sun 9am–8pm; www.ursula.fi) is a Helsinki institution. Stop for coffee and cake, and of course to linger on the canopied terrace, with its stunning views of Suomenlinna and the other small islands offshore.

Café Ursula offers cake and fabulous sea views

KALLIO AND AROUND

Ten minutes' walk from the ceaseless crowds at the Central Railway Station is an oasis of green tranquility. **Helsinki University Botanical Gardens** ㊳ (Unioninkatu 44, tel: 09 1912 4455; www.luomus.fi; garden, daily 9am–8pm; free; greenhouses, Tues–Sun 10am–5pm, Thur until 6pm June–Aug, to 4pm, Thur until 6pm Sept–May; charge) was actually established in Turku, and transferred to Helsinki's venerable Kaisaniemi Park in 1829. It consists of a formal garden with several 1830s Empire-style buildings and a series of greenhouses, the largest of which is the 1889 Palm House. The plants – nearly 3,000 varieties – are grouped according to their family or origin; they are labelled white for basic plants, red for endangered ones, and yellow for edible and medicinal types.

Crossing over the Long Bridge – actually rather short – at the north side of the park brings you into the interesting, working-class area of **Kallio**.

HAKANIEMI MARKET

To the left of McDonald's you will see the statue of *The Boxers* by Johannes Haapasalo, and in the large square to the right is **Hakaniemi Market** ❸ (Mon–Sat 6.30am–3pm), with an enticing array of products ranging from vegetables and fish to wicker furniture. There are also some of the small, tented cafés that are so popular across Finland. The two-storey **Market Hall** (Mon–Fri 8am–6pm, Sat 8am–4pm; www.hakaniemenkauppa halli.fi) has food on the lower level, and an array of textiles and souvenirs upstairs. Unlike the Old Market Hall by Market Square, this one caters more to local people than to tourists.

KALLIO CHURCH

The most dominant landmark is straight ahead on top of the hill, reached by the longest street in Helsinki, Siltasaarenkatu.

Before starting the climb, note the unusual memorial to the left at the first intersection. It consists of a leaning 8m (26 ft) steel tower and a 7.5m (24.5 ft) slab of grey Kuru granite, with reliefs depicting women at work in homes, factories and farms, and is the first national memorial honouring the work done by women during World War II.

Kallio in film

Director Aki Kaurismäki plays with the realities and stereotypes of the working-class Kallio district in some of his films, most notably *Calamari Union* (1985), where 14 men named Frank set off on a deadly journey from Kallio to Eira, an up-market neighbourhood in the south of the city.

The tall, granite, Art Nouveau tower of **Kallio Church** ⓪ (Kallion kikko, www.helsinginkirkot.fi; Mon–Fri 7am–9pm, Sat–Sun 9am–7pm) is most impressive, and sits on one of Helsinki's highest spots. Consecrated on 1 September 1912, it is the only church in Finland that has both baroque and French Romantic organs. It also has seven bells, and Sibelius composed a melody specially for them; it was used by the Finnish Broadcasting Company for a number of decades, when they were rung on Saturday evening.

In the morning (except on Sundays) you may see a queue of people along Castréninkatu, behind the church. They are lining up for free bread from the Salvation Army. On the whole, Finland is an affluent country, but pockets of poverty do exist, and this is one of them.

SÖRNÄINEN

Areas of the industrial Sörnäinen district, northeast of Kallio, are being slowly transformed into cultural spaces. The city's municipal abattoir **Teurastamo** (www.teurastamo.com) served as a wholesale farmers market after the last cow was slaughtered there in 1992, and is now being developed as a foodie area. Its austere redbrick buildings, dating back to 1933, house several restaurants, a flavour laboratory and the little **Jädelino ice cream factory** (tel: 040 350 3773; www.jadelino.fi; Mon–Sat 11am–8pm).

The former power station **Suvilahti** makes an epic backdrop for rock and metal gigs, such as the Tuska Open-Air Metal Festival (www.tuska-festival.fi) held at the end of June. Its old industrial units are being rented out to various cultural groups as office and exhibition spaces. **Cirko – Centre for New Circus** (www.cirko.fi), based in a former gasworks, has a year-round programme of contemporary Finnish circus performances. Kalasatama metro station is right next door to the power station.

LENININPUISTO AND LINNANMÄKI

Lenininpuisto is a pleasant little park with a much broader array of trees and shrubs than you would normally find in a Finnish garden, the result of a garden exhibition that was held here in 1961–62. The park was originally named Alpine Park (Alppipuisto), but was given a new moniker in 1970, the 100th anniversary of Vladimir Ilyich Lenin's birth, as a friendly nod to the Soviet Union.

Helsinki's amusement park, **Linnanmäki** 41 (tel: 010-5722 200; May–mid-Oct: days and times vary – see website for details; www.linnanmaki.fi), is perched on top of a wooded hill. Half a million people visit every year, attracted by its rides and sideshows, from an old-fashioned carousel to the famous wooden rollercoaster Vuoristorata to up-to-date rides like the

Flow Festival in Suvilahti

75m- (246 ft-) tall freefall tower Kingi. A few of the rides are free; an all-ride pass costs €35, with profits going to children's charities.

You can also buy a joint ticket (€47) that covers entry to Linnanmäki and its neighbour, **Sea Life Helsinki** (tel: 09-565 8200; May–Aug daily 10am–7pm, June and July until 8pm; Sept–Apr Mon–Tues and Thur–Sun 10am–5pm, Wed 10am–7pm; charge; www.visitsealife.com/helsinki). The Sea Life centre is fairly small, but it has been extremely well designed and the staff are knowledgeable. Feeding times take place on the hour – check details as you enter.

If you have small children whose legs need a rest, Linnanmäki and Sea Life Helsinki are served by tram Nos 3 and 9, and bus No. 23, from the Central Railway Station.

SUOMENLINNA FORTRESS

Suomenlinna Fortress ㊷ is one of the biggest sea forts in the world, with fortifications scattered across eight rocky skerries. It is Helsinki's top attraction, as well as being a Unesco World Heritage Site, and deserves a full day to explore. The municipal HSL ferry departs year-round from Market Square, landing at the Main Quay on the north side of Iso Mustasaari island. It is supplemented in summer by JT-Line's waterbus, which also departs from Market Square, landing at the Suomenlinna Centre pier on the south of Iso Mustasaari, and at King's Gate on Kustaanmiekka. The ferry ride takes 15 to 20 minutes.

The **Suomenlinna Centre** (May–Sept daily 10am–6pm, Oct–Apr daily 10.30am–4.30pm; www.suomenlinna.fi), on the south of Iso Mustasaari, is the place to pick up a copy of the colourful and practical guide to the islands, or to join one of the guided tours (in English at 11am, 12.30pm and 2.30pm daily

June–Aug, 1.30pm Sat and Sun Oct–May). There is also a **visitor centre** (tel: 029 533 8410; May–Sept daily 10am–6pm, Oct–Apr daily 10am–4pm) at the Main Quay, with brochures and an introductory exhibition.

Some paths are rather rough and difficult to access with wheelchairs or children's pushchairs – the visitor centre can also provide a map of routes suitable for those with impaired mobility. A torch will come in handy if you want to explore some of the tunnels that run underneath the fortification. Bring a swimsuit too, as there are several sheltered coves with little sandy beaches.

There are 12 cafés and restaurants on the islands, although some are summer only. For restaurants, see page 110. Café Piper (tel: 09-668 447; daily late May 10am–5pm, June–mid-Aug

The impressive Suomenlinna Fortress

10am–7pm, mid-Aug–mid-Sept 11am–5pm), in a park just south of the Ehrensvärd Crown Castle, offers alfresco dining with a stunning view.

Accommodation on the island is limited to Hostel Suomenlinna (see page 141).

CONSTRUCTION OF THE FORTRESS

By the middle of the 17th century Sweden had become one of the great European powers. However, this predominance began to slip after 1703, when Peter the Great founded the new Russian capital of St Petersburg and fortified its approaches with the naval base of Kronstadt. Successive wars saw Sweden lose much of its Baltic territories, and, through the treaties of Nystad and Turku, the Russian frontier was brought much closer, posing more of a threat. In 1748, the Swedish Diet decided to build a new naval base to protect Helsinki's shipping channels and serve as a landing base for extra troops from Sweden.

The new fortress, occupying a series of small islands outside Helsinki harbour, was called Sveaborg – Sweden's Fortress – and became the largest construction project ever undertaken by the country. Lieutenant-Colonel Augustin Ehrensvärd (1710–72), an astute politician and experienced fortress planner, had the responsibility of overseeing the construction. He decided that, to keep the edifice hidden as much as possible from enemy view, it should be a bastion with low fortification devices. It took many thousands of Finnish workers some 40 years to complete the principal work – by which time the walls extended to a total of around 8km (5 miles), with enough room for 1,300 cannons.

MILITARY ACTION

By 1806, around 4,600 people were living on Sveaborg (Suomenlinna), making it the second-largest city in Finland after Turku. In 1809, Finland became an autonomous duchy within the Russian Empire, ending the 600-year period of Swedish rule. It was the presence of this fortress that prompted the Russians to make Helsinki the new Finnish capital in 1812.

A period of peace followed. However, this was shattered by the Crimean War of 1854–56, during which an Anglo-French fleet shelled and badly damaged the fortress over a period of three days. After the war, extensive restoration work was undertaken, with new defensive work on the western and southern edges of the islands. In the build up to World War I the fortress and surrounding islands were incorporated into naval fortifications designed to protect St Petersburg.

After Finland gained its independence, Sveaborg was given its new name, Suomenlinna or "Finland's Fortress". Its first, grisly use was as a death camp for the Reds (communists) who had lost the Finnish Civil War. It was then utilised as a closed military zone until 1948, and it was not until 1973 that Suomenlinna received a civilian administration. In 1991 the fortress became a Unesco World Heritage Site, for its unique and excellently preserved military architecture.

ARTISTIC ENCLAVE

Despite its military purpose, Suomenlinna has always been known as a place of avant-garde culture, where the arts, music and theatre have flourished, an environment assisted by the large numbers of officers stationed there. Augustin Ehrensvärd himself had a passion for art, having studied painting, drawing and engraving in Paris in his 20s.

Today, many artists live permanently on Suomenlinna. There are a number of studios and galleries on the islands, including the Pot Viapori Ceramic Studio and the Hytti Glass Studio, where you can watch glass being blown. The three-day craft-focused Väkevä Viapori village fete is held in late October. Music and theatre also flourish: Suomenlinna has a vibrant jazz festival, the summertime Viapori Jazz (http://viaporijazz.fi), and the open-air summer theatre staged at the bastion of Hyvä Omatunto – meaning Good Conscience – regularly has sell-out performances.

There are around 800 civilians living on the islands now, of whom about 400 work here year round, while the rest commute to Helsinki. They all enjoy a privileged position, being close to the centre of Helsinki yet removed from city stresses on their own idyllic islands.

SUOMENLINNA'S MUSEUMS

A visit to Suomenlinna is also enhanced by its collection of six museums, five of which are open only in summer. From June to August, you can purchase a combined admission ticket.

The most important is **Suomenlinna Museum** (Building C74, tel: 09-684 1850; May–Sept daily 10am–6pm; Oct–Apr daily 10.30am–4.30pm; charge). Located in the navy's former inventory chambers, it doubles as an information centre and details the history of the fortress from the 18th century to the present. Don't miss the interesting multimedia show, 'The Suomenlinna Experience', broadcast every half hour in the auditorium.

One of the oldest houses in the complex is the former Commandant's official residence, part home, part defensive structure – the crenel-lated dining-room window and sleeping alcove could be used to defend the fortress's main entrance in emergencies. It now houses the **Ehrensvärd Museum** (Building B40, tel: 09-684 1850; June–Aug daily 10am–5pm, late May and early Sept daily 11am–4pm; charge), containing portraits, furnishings and model ships. Ehrensvärd himself is buried in front of the house, his final rest-

Suomenlinna artist at work

ing place marked by an elaborate grave topped with a sword, shield and helmet that was designed by his godson, King Gustav III of Sweden.

The Military Museum has two separate entities. The **Manege** (Maneesi; Building C77, tel: 0299 530 261; May–Sept daily 11am–6pm; charge) features heavy military equipment – most of which dates from the World War II era – in an artillery store-house constructed by the Russians in 1881. The **Submarine Vesikko** (*Sukellusvene Vesikko*; Building B79, tel: 0 299 530 260; early-May–Sept daily 11am–6pm; charge), which patrolled the Gulf of Finland during the Winter and Continuation Wars, is the Finnish Navy's only surviving WWII submarine.

A more gentle experience can be found at the **Toy Museum** (Lelumuseo; Building C66, tel: 040 500 6607; June–Aug 11am–6pm, late April–mid-May and Sept weekends only, check web-site for times; charge; www.lelumuseo.fi) where, in an old

Submarine Vesikko

Russian villa, there is a collection of dolls and toys dating from the 1830s onwards. There's also a small café, should you need a break for refreshment.

The tiny **Customs Museum** (Building B20 D, tel: 040 332 2774; June–Aug Tues–Sun 12.30pm–5.30pm; free) on Susisaari has an exhibition on customs and smuggling.

SUOMENLINNA CHURCH

Not to be missed is **Suomenlinna Church** (Suomenlinnan kirkko; summer Tues 11.30am–1.30pm, Thur–Sun noon–4pm), which was inaugurated in 1854 as the Alexander Nevsky Orthodox Church. Originally, it had five towers with onion domes but when, in 1928, it changed alliances and became a Lutheran church, four of the towers were demolished and the main one rebuilt in more fitting style. Its bell is the largest in Finland and the fence, made of cannon and chains, was erected in the 1850s.

The church is popular for summer weddings, and also functions as a lighthouse.

HELSINKI'S ISLANDS

Hundreds of islands dot the city's coastline. Some, like Lauttasaari and Kulosaari, have been so integrated by bridges and metro lines that they are almost indistinguishable from the mainland. Others are private, reserved for weekend cottages, reached over the ice in winter or by motorboat in summer. But others are recreational areas, open to all – the most famous being the great fortifications of Suomenlinna. Below are some other good choices.

SEURASAARI

A must-see sight, Seurasaari is a beautiful green park-like island, attached to the mainland by a wooden footbridge. You could spend a very happy afternoon here, exploring the appealing **Seurasaari Open-Air Museum** ⓧ (tel: 0295 33 6912; Jun–Aug daily 11am–5pm; late May and early Sept Mon–Fri 9am–3pm, Sat–Sun 11am–5pm; charge) and its forested surroundings. The museum was founded in 1909 and has 86 traditional buildings – cottages, farmsteads, a church and parsonage and a manor house – relocated from all Finland's provinces, which give visitors an engaging perspective of Finnish rural life from the 18th to the 20th century. Guides in traditional costumes demonstrate craft skills and folk dancing, and an optional guided tour (in English at 3pm) is included in the ticket price. Helsinki's main Midsummer's Eve celebrations take place here in June: the national flag flutters over traditional dancers, a merry wedding and a huge bonfire. A bonfire is also lit here on Easter Saturday, to drive away witches and evil spirits, who are said to be particularly active on that day.

Saaristo, one of many island-restaurants

On the western side of the island is the pretty **Seurasaari Beach**, created in 1906. It mainly functions as a naturist beach, with separate areas for women and men, but swimsuits are compulsory on Wednesday and Sunday.

Bus No. 24 runs to Seurasaari from the western end of Esplanadi. The pleasant route takes you around the waterside, past Sibelius Park, and gives you a glimpse of **Mäntyniemi**, the official residence of the Finnish president.

KORKEASAARI

Korkeasaari, a rocky outcrop offshore from the Mustikkamaa district of Helsinki, has served time as farmland, a timber store and as a military zone, but since 1889, it has been the home of **Helsinki Zoo** ㉔ (Högholmen; tel: 09-310 37900; daily May–Aug 10am–8pm, Apr and Sept until 6pm, Oct–Mar until 4pm; charge; www.korkeasaari.fi). Perhaps not surprisingly, this popular tourist attraction specialises in "cold climate animals", including some big beasts like Asian lions, brown bear and snow leopards – the zoo has a very successful breeding programme for the latter. The interesting Amazonia House enclosure is home to South American animals. Bus No. 16 runs from the Central Railway Station year round; but if you're here in summer, it's great fun to go by boat. A service runs daily from Market Square May to September, and the Hakaniemi ferry runs daily from the Kallio district from June to August.

PIHLAJASAARI

Helsinki's favourite island for swimming is undoubtedly **Pihlajasaari** ("Rowan Island"), actually two islands joined by a bridge. You'll find a sandy beach, café, sauna and changing cabins on the larger island's western shore. The mixed naturist beach is on the smaller island, which also hides wartime bunkers. Pihlajasaari is just a 10-minute trip from the mainland. Boats depart from mid-May to August every 15 to 30 minutes, from outside Café Carusel, at the western edge of Kaivopuisto Park. Weekend camping is permitted.

HARAKKA

"Magpie island" is now a wildlife reserve but, up until 1990, was reserved for military purposes; this helps explain why it is still so pristine. A network of paths (marked by signposts giving information in Finnish and Swedish) circle the tiny island, and visitors are asked not to stray from these paths or remove plants. There's lots of birdlife here, and an art centre with artists' studios. You can reach Harakka by boat in summer: to summon your craft, hoist the red-and-white wooden signal at the end of the pier, near to Café Ursula in Kaivopuisto Park, and a boat should arrive within half an hour.

Helsinki Zoo brown bear

GREATER HELSINKI

The Capital and Greater Helsinki areas spread out in a concentric fan shape around the central city. Their quiet commuter towns and suburbs hide several interesting sights.

TARVASPÄÄ

Akseli Gallén-Kallela (1865–1931) is considered by many to be Finland's greatest national artist. After studying at the Finnish Society of Fine Arts, he made his debut in the 1880s to popular acclaim, with his realistic images of everyday Finns. Gallén-Kallela became fascinated with Elias Lönnrot's epic poetry collection, the Kalevala, even honeymooning in the regions where the folk poems originated. His rich, romantic paintings revisit the poems' mythical heroes and their stories over and over again.

Gallén-Kallela designed and built a studio-home, **Tarvaspää** (1911–13), overlooking Laajalahti Bay 10km (6.2 miles) west of Helsinki, bringing to life his dream of "a crenellated castle, with a tower of grey stone and timbers of pine and oak". His studio has been converted into the **Gallén-Kallela Museum** (Gallén-Kallenlatie 27; tel: 09-849 2340; www.gallen-kallela. fi; mid-May–Aug daily 11am–6pm, Sept–mid-May Tues–Sat 11am–4pm, Sun 11am–5pm; charge; guided tours by arrangement), a peaceful oasis consisting of a studio wing, tower and main building, with a coffee house and a terrace restaurant. The museum holds some 100 illustrations for the *Kalevala*, which decorated the Finnish Pavilion at the Paris World Exhibition in 1900; the paintings themselves can be seen at the Ateneum in Helsinki (see page 28).

Tram No. 4 runs nearby from central Helsinki: get off at Laajalahden aukio and enjoy the scenic 2km (1-mile) walk to the museum through Munkinpuisto Park.

ESPOO

Populated largely by wealthier Finns who commute to Helsinki, Espoo is a strange mix of rural farm areas and genteel, leafy suburbs that offer a large and colourful palette of Finnish residential architectural styles. It is actually Finland's second-largest city, although it feels a planet away from the Londons or Tokyos of this world. In particular, Espoo's **Tapiola** area, named after Tapio, the *Kalevala*'s spirit of the forest, is a renowned 1950s and 1960s planned garden suburb. Leading architects of the age aimed to create a harmonious mix of housing, cultural and recreational facilities, set around a central pool. **Espoo Cultural Centre** (Espoon kulttuurikeskus), home to the city's orchestra and theatre, and host of the big April Jazz Festival, sits at its heart. The white quartzite, concrete and glass complex was created in 1972 by Arto Sipinen, who worked with Alvar Aalto and has designed monumental-style civic works in the same tradition.

Another of Espoo's assets is **WeeGee** (tel: 09-816 31818; Tues, Thur 11am–6pm, Wed, Fri 11am–7pm, Sat–Sun 11am–5pm; charge; www.weegee.fi), a clutch of five museums gathered inside an atmospheric old printing works. The best-known is **EMMA** (www.emma.museum), with around 2500 Finnish art works dating from the 1950s onwards. Finland's largest collection of West African objects, gathered by the radio and television reporter Helinä Rautavaara, can be seen in the interesting **ethnographic museum** (http://helinamuseo.fi), and the **Finnish Toy Museum** (Suomen Lelumuseo Hevosenkenkä; www.lelumuseohevosenkenka.fi) is also worth a look.

NUUKSIO NATIONAL PARK

Finns have a passion for the outdoors, and much of the Finnish landscape is safeguarded by 38 varied national parks. Just 16km (10 miles) north of Espoo is **Nuuksio National Park** (Nuuksion kansallispuisto; www.nationalparks.fi), a great place to come for a short hiking trip of a day or two. The park is one of the most important conservation areas in Finland, with cool, herb-rich forests, lakes and mires that are home to a number of threatened species, including the wood lark, European nightjar and various flying squirrels. Around 33km (20 miles) of marked trails thread through the area, and many companies offer activities such as fishing, canoeing and mushroom-picking in summer, and guided snow shoe walking and skiing excursions in winter – see the national park website for a full list of providers.

The award-winning **Finnish Nature Centre Haltia** (tel: 040-163 6200; May–Sept 10am–6pm, Oct–Apr Tue–Sat 10am–5pm;

charge for exhibition; www.haltia.com) has exhibitions on Finnish nature if you are not able to get out into the forest itself.

You can reach the park's eastern/northern trails from the centre of Espoo via bus 85(A); and southern sections via bus 28 from Leppävaara in Espoo. In summer, a bus also runs from Helsinki – ask the tourist office for information.

HVITTRÄSK

Hvitträsk (tel: 0295 33 6952; May–Sept daily 11am–5pm, Oct–Apr Wed–Sun 11am–5pm; charge; guided tours in May Sat–Sun, June–Sept Wed–Sun at 3pm), some 20km (14 miles) west of Helsinki in Kirkkonummi municipality, is another must-see mecca for anyone interested in Finnish art, architecture and design.

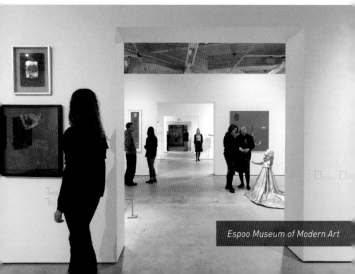

Espoo Museum of Modern Art

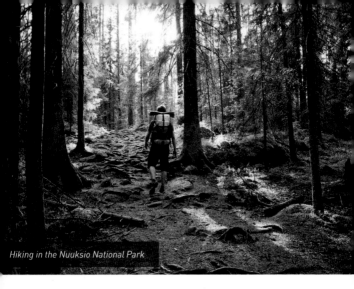

Hiking in the Nuuksio National Park

Eliel Saarinen, Herman Gesellius and Armas Lindgren were three of Finland's most famous architects, responsible for many of Helsinki's most unusual and important buildings. Together they designed this studio home, where all three lived and worked. The stone and timber buildings, built in National Romantic style between 1901 and 1903, blend into the forest and cliffs, while the interior architecture, furniture and design form a harmonious whole.

Harmony of design did not always extend into the private lives of the little community, however. Saarinen's first wife, Matilda, crossed the garden to live with his partner, Gesellius. Apparently bearing her no grudge, Saarinen married Gesellius' sister, Loja, two years later. But the triumvirate broke up in 1906, and by 1916 Saarinen was working at Hvitträsk on his own. In 1922, after winning a major prize in a competition in New York, Saarinen moved to the United States, becoming as well known abroad as he was in Finland. He continued to visit Hvitträsk each year until his death in 1950, and his grave overlooks the lake that gave the house its name.

Hvitträsk can be reached by train (L or U train: Helsinki–Luoma; 3km/2-mile walk).

EXCURSIONS

Helsinki is a small capital city: once you have seen its sights, take a day trip to soak up Finland's countryside; visit an atmospheric medieval trading town; or hop across the water to explore Tallinn, a Unesco World Heritage Site.

FISKARS

This attractive 17th-century ironworking village (*bruk*) makes for a very popular shopping/sightseeing trip from Helsinki. The village is where the Fiskars company, makers of the iconic orange-handled tools, was born. A chuckling river runs in front of a long street of pretty buildings, many designed by Engel himself. Today they form a concentrated pocket of Finnish art and design. Their little outlets, selling pottery, glassware, paper, leather goods, homeware, jewellery, clothing, chocolates and artisanal beer, open from 11am to 5pm in summer (weekends only during the rest of the year).

The Engel-designed **Clock Tower** building is the centrepiece of the village, containing an exhibition about the Fiskars company and a shop selling Fiskars products. Downriver, you'll find the 19th-century **copper forge** and **Assembly Hall**; while upstream near the lake is **Fiskars Museum** (Peltorivi 9, tel: 019 237 013; Apr–May, Sept–mid-Jan Wed–Sun 11am–5pm, June–Aug daily 11am–5pm; charge; www.fiskarsmuseum.fi), a living-history museum, where costumed workers bring the village's ironworking history to life.

Mainly, the chief pleasure here lies in soaking up the charming atmosphere, wandering in and out of the studios and workshops, and stopping for cakes and coffee at one of the riverside cafés.

Getting There

Fiskars is 88km (55 miles) west of Helsinki. Take the InterCity Helsinki–Turku train, and get off in Karjaa, from where the village is a 20-minute bus ride (weekdays).

PORVOO (BORGÅ)

Finland's second-oldest town was once an affluent medieval trading centre, and many of its picturesque old buildings, including the ochre-red shore houses, have been preserved. Besides its fine cathedral, sitting majestically on the hill between the Market Square and the riverside, the town has several interesting museums and speciality shops. Visit the **tourist office** (Läntinen Aleksanterinkatu 1; tel: 040 489 9801; Mon–Fri 9am–6pm, Sat 11am–4pm; www.visitporvoo.fi), based in the new Art Factory conference centre, to stock up on information.

The **Old Town** is a highlight of a visit to Porvoo. Down by the river, Jokikatu is a small, cobbled street with attractive wooden buildings housing an array

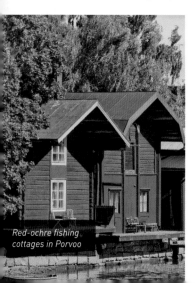
Red-ochre fishing cottages in Porvoo

Colourful Porvoo

of craft and souvenir shops. It is here that you really feel the ambience of this unusual little town, especially beside the old shore houses and granary buildings that back onto the river. One of these granaries now contains the **Porvoo Doll and Toy Museum** (tel: 040-501 5006; Jun–mid-Aug daily 10am–3pm; charge; www.lelumuseo.com), consisting of over 1,000 dolls and hundreds of toys collected from Finland and abroad. It is generally considered the best collection of its kind in the country.

The square, rococo-style Old Town Hall (1764), with an unusual central tower, is one of only two 18th-century town halls remaining in Finland. It contains works by two Porvoo natives, artist Albert Edelfelt (1854–1905) and the sculptor Ville Vallgren (1855–1940), who went on to win international fame – Vallgren's most famous work is the statue *Havis Amanda* (see page 29) in Helsinki. The rest of **Porvoo Museum** (tel: 040 197 5557; May–Aug Mon–Sat 10am–4pm, Sun 11am–4pm;

Sept–Apr Wed–Sun noon–4pm; charge; www.porvoonmuseo.fi), detailing bygone times with displays of costumes, textiles, glass, porcelain and silver, is in the neighbouring Holm House.

Steep, cobbled Sillanmäki – difficult for cars and pedestrians alike – leads up to one of Finland's loveliest Gothic churches, **Porvoo Cathedral** (Tuomiokirkko; tel: 019-661 1250; May–Sept Mon–Fri 10am–6pm, Sat 10am–2pm, Sun 2–5pm; Oct–Apr Tues–Sat 10am–2pm, Sun 2–4pm; www.porvoonseurakunnat.fi). Following Russia's defeat of Sweden, the Diet of Porvoo (1809), which established Finland as a Grand Duchy belonging to Russia, was held here. Dating mainly from the 15th century, the building has had many near misses over the centuries, most notably when it was hit by a bomb in World War II and damaged by arson in 2006. Points of interest include a statue of Alexander I, erected in 1909 on the centenary of the Porvoo Diet, and the cathedral's separate bell tower.

Finland's national poet J. L. Runeberg (1804–77) was a local lad – the town still celebrates his birthday on 5th February with an annual torchlight parade and jam-topped Runeberg tarts. On the other side of town, in a grid of Empire-style houses, you'll find Finland's oldest home museum, the **J. L. Runeberg Home** (tel: 040 489 9900; May–Aug daily 10am–4pm; Sept–Apr Wed–Sun 10am–4pm; charge). Runeberg and his family lived here for 25 years. In 1882 the building was opened as a museum, and the interior remains unchanged from that time.

Getting There

Porvoo is 50km (32 miles) east of Helsinki. There are bus services every half hour, departing from Kamppi bus station in Helsinki, taking around an hour.

If you prefer to go by boat, the *J. L. Runeberg* (tel: 019 524 3331, www.msjlruneberg.fi) sails in summer from Helsinki

Market Square, leaving at 10am and returning at 4pm, allowing around 2.5 to 3 hours' sightseeing in Porvoo. It.sets sail every day except Thursday in July and Tue–Wed, Fri–Sun on June and August (some other sailings available in May), with the return journey costing €39.

TALLINN, ESTONIA

Helsinki's central position on the Gulf of Finland makes it an excellent jumping-off point for visits to other Baltic cities. Tallinn, the capital of Estonia, is the closest, just a 1.5-hour hop across the water. It is a popular destination for Finns, drawn by its lively nightlife. Tallinn's prosperity was built up during the 13th to 16th centuries, when it was the northernmost member of the Hanseatic trading league. Despite the centuries of turmoil that followed, the Old Town has survived relatively unscathed. A living medieval monument, it was made a Unesco World Heritage Site in 1997.

Tallinn

To get a sense of the city, join the **Tallinn Free Tour**, which departs at noon daily from outside the tourist office at Niguliste 2.

Raekoda Plats

Town Hall Square (Raekoda plats) has been Tallinn's marketplace and social centre for more than seven centuries.

Dominating it is the **Raekoda**, the oldest intact Gothic town hall in Northern Europe. Its eight-sided **tower** (tel: 645 7900; http://raekoda.tallinn.ee; May–mid-Sept daily 11am–6pm; charge) has a viewing platform offering spectacular views. The **Old Thomas** (Vana Toomas) weathervane at the top of the tower was added in 1530.

Numerous interesting buildings line the square, and its cafés and restaurants are ideal places to soak up the city's engaging ambience. The **Balthasar**, Raekoja plats 11, is Estonia's "first garlic restaurant", and even offers ice cream with honey and garlic sauce. It's in the same ancient building as Europe's oldest **Chemist Shop** (tel: 631 4860; www.raeapteek.ee; Mon–Sat 9am–6pm), founded in 1422, which sells a marzipan concoction said to relieve the pain of love.

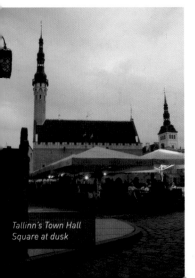

Tallinn's Town Hall Square at dusk

Church of the Holy Ghost

Just off the square, the **Church of the Holy Ghost** (tel: 644 1487; www.puhavaimu.ee; May–Sept Mon–Sat 9am–6pm, Sun between services, rest of year shorter, varied hours; charge) is easily identifiable by the attractive old clock – Tallinn's oldest – on its façade. The church dates from the 14th century, and was built by the Order of the Holy Ghost. After the Reformation, the first sermons in the

Estonian language were given here. The interior is richly decorated, and includes one of the most precious medieval works of art in the country, an altar dating from 1483.

The church is almost on the corner of Pikk, a nice little street with an array of colourful stone houses. Particularly grand is the 16th-century **House of the Brotherhood of Blackheads** (tel: 6699 947; www.mustpeademaja.ee), a guild for unmarried merchants. Today it is a popular concert venue.

At the junction with Pagari, the formidable building with bricked-up basement windows was the headquarters of the NKWD – better known by its later name, the KGB. Here, suspected enemies of the Soviet Union were interrogated, then shot or sent to Siberian work camps.

City Walls and the Cathedral

The Square of Towers Park has the best views of the formidable **City Walls** (Tallinna Linnaamüür). The walls encompassed 2.5km (1.5 miles), and about 75 percent still stand today. In the Middle Ages, there were six gates and no fewer than 66 towers. Today 19 survive: the ones in this stretch are oddly shaped, and topped by irregular, conical, red-tiled roofs. Climb the nearby **Nun's Tower** (Nunna torn; tel: 644 9867; June–Aug daily 11am–7pm; Apr–May and Sept–Oct Fri–Wed 11am–5pm, Nov–Mar Fri–Tue 11am–4pm; charge) and cross the wooden platform towards the Bath Tower and Golden Leg Tower (*Sauna* and *Kuldjala*).

On Castle Square (Lossi plats), **St Alexander Nevsky Cathedral** (tel: 644 3484; Sun–Fri 8am–7pm, Sat 8am–8pm; free) looms over the area, dominated by five unmistakable onion domes. Named in honour of the Russian duke who attacked southeastern Estonia in the first part of the 13th century, the cathedral was constructed between 1894 and 1900 on the orders of Tsar Alexander III. The bell tower contains Tallinn's grandest collection of bells, the largest weighing 15 tonnes; the entire ensemble is played before each service.

Toompea Castle

Opposite the cathedral's main entrance is the pink baroque façade of **Toompea Castle**, emblazoned with the city's coat of arms – three lions on a gold background. From this angle, most of what you can see is 18th-century stonework; however, the first fortress on the site dates from the early 13th century. The dominant feature of the castle is the battlemented, 46m (151ft) 14th-century tower on the southwestern corner. Called **Pikk Hermann** (Tall Hermann), it is the symbol of Tallinn. After a 50-year Russian occupation, the blue, black and white tricolour, the national flag of Estonia, was raised here once again in 1991.

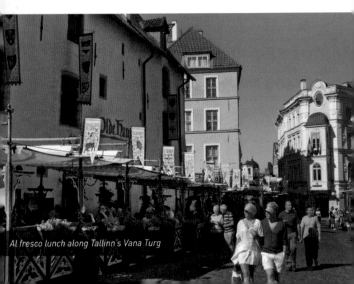

Al fresco lunch along Tallinn's Vana Turg

Take Toom-Kooli – between the cathedral and the castle – to the **Dome Church** (Toomkirk; tel: 644 4140; Tue–Sun 10am–4.30pm; free). It dates from the time of the first Danish invaders in the 13th century, when it was just a wooden hall, dedicated to St Mary the Virgin. It is the oldest church on mainland Estonia, and the country's primary Lutheran church. The Gothic exterior dates from the 14th century.

Toompea Castle

The Danish King's Garden

The **Danish King's Garden** (Taani Kuninga aed), a little park inside the walls, is home to two impressive towers – **Neitsitorn** and **Kiek in de Kök** (tel: 644 6686; Mar–Oct Tues–Sun 10.30am–6pm, Nov–Feb Tues–Sun 10am–5.30pm; charge; http://linnamuuseum. ee). The latter contains an interesting museum, sketching out the history of the city, and is also the place to book a tour of the **Bastion Tunnels** that run under the city's fortifications.

Getting There

Ferries to Tallinn take about two hours with **Tallink Silja** (in Helsinki, tel: +358 9 180 41, www.tallinksilja.com; in Tallinn, tel: +372 640 9808), with at least six departures per day. By making an early start you can cram Tallinn's most important sites into a day, but an overnight stay will allow for a more leisurely exploration.

Saunas are generally same sex only; only mixed ones are either for families or groups of close friends

WHAT TO DO

ENTERTAINMENT

Helsinki is full of music. Whether you enjoy classical concerts, or headbanging to heavy metal, or something in between, the city has something for you. State-of-the-art auditoriums host orchestras and operas; choral music crescendos in the city's churches; two distinguished theatres entertain in both Finnish and Swedish; and live music fills the city's pubs and clubs.

Helsinki may not have the biggest bar scene on earth, but its nightlife is friendly, vibrant and inclusive. Quirky pubs, designer bars, laidback jazz joints and wild nightclubs will keep you partying your way across town until the early hours.

Two national parks lie on Helsinki's doorstep, full of opportunities for outdoor activities and wildlife watching. Within the city, you can canoe, experience a Finnish sauna, sunbathe at the beach, or enjoy the passionate atmosphere at an ice hockey match.

CONCERT AND THEATRE TICKETS

Tickets can be booked through the following ticket agencies:

Lippupalvelu (Mannerheimintie 13 a A; tel: 0600 10 800 – local call charge plus €1.98 per minute; open Mon–Fri 9am–6pm, Sat 10am–5pm; www.lippupalvelu.fi)

Lippupiste (Luckan Forum, Simonsgatan 8; tel: 0600 900 900 – local call charge plus €1.98 per minute; open Mon, Wed, Fri 11am–5pm, Tue, Thur 11am–7pm, Sat noon–3pm; www.lippu.fi)

Tiketti (Aleksanterinkatu 52; tel: 0600 1 1616 – local call charge plus €1.78 per minute; open Mon–Fri 9am–9pm, Sat until 7pm, Sun 11am–6pm; www.tiketti.fi)

Mussikkitalo design

The seating in the Music Centre's main concert hall mimics logs floating down a Finnish river, while the traditional Finnish smoke sauna is conjured up in the auditorium's stained-birch woodwork.

MUSIC AND THEATRE

Finland has a lively **classical music** scene, with a disproportionately high number of world-class composers, conductors and performers. The state-of-the-art **Helsinki Music Centre** (Musiikkitalo; tel: 020 707 0400; www.musiikkitalo.fi) is Helsinki's newest music venue and home of the prestigious Sibelius Academy (www.siba.fi), the Finnish Radio Symphony Orchestra (www.yle.fi/rso) and the Helsinki Philharmonic Orchestra. The centre hosts up to 100 concerts per month between September and May, from orchestral works to rock gigs.

The **Rock Church** (Temppeliaukio; Lutherinkatu 3; opening hours on tel. 09 2340 5940), hewn from solid bedrock, also has amazing acoustics. Chamber concerts, and jazz, choir and piano recitals are held here; performances of Sibelius's work are especially popular. Contact the tourist office for upcoming events.

Finland has a long-standing love affair with opera. The **Finnish National Opera** (Helsinginkatu 58; tel: 09 4030 2211; www.opera.fi) stages around 15 classic and contemporary operas per season (September to May), plus nine ballets.

Kulttuuritalo (Sturenkatu 4; tel: 09 774 0270; www.kulttuuritalo.fi), opened in 1958, was architect Alvar Aalto's first public building in Helsinki. The asymmetrical auditorium has some of the best acoustics in the country, and hosts a year-round programme of pop, rock and classical concerts, and stand-up comedy shows.

The modern **Hartwall Arena** (Areenakuja 1; tel. 204 1997

www.hartwallarena.fi), with its own dedicated railway station, hosts major sporting events, shows and rock gigs. Purchase tickets from Lippupiste.

Finland's **UMO Jazz Orchestra** (www.umo.fi), a Finnish Big Band with 26 albums to its name, plays everything from boogie to the blues. The orchestra performs around 80 concerts per year at venues across the country and abroad – check the website for details. One of Europe's best jazz clubs, **Happy Jazz Club Storyville** (Museokatu 8; tel: 50 363 2664; www.storyville. fi) is an ever-popular Helsinki nightspot. Close to the parliament building, in an old coal cellar, you'll find live jazz from 7pm until the early hours Wednesday to Saturday. The ground-floor Piano Bar opens Tuesday to Saturday from 6pm, and in summer there is daily live music on the delightful Garden Terrace.

Outdoor classical concert in Esplanade Park

The **Finnish National Theatre** (Läntinen teatterikuja 1; tel: 10 733 1331; www.nationaltheatre.fi) and the **Swedish Theatre** (Svenska Teatern; Pohjoisesplanadi 2; tel: 09 6162 1411; www. svenskateatern.fi) both enjoy long traditions of performance in, respectively, Finnish and Swedish. The National Theatre has English surtitles for some performances.

CINEMA

Finns do not dub foreign films, so you can enjoy newly released Hollywood movies at the 10-screen **Kinopalatsi** in Kaisaniemenkatu 2, and at Finland's most high-tech cinema, the 14-screen **Tennispalatsi** at Salomonkatu 15. Cinema listings can be found at the kiosk outside the east entrance to Helsinki railway station; in newspapers; at the tourist office; and at the Finnkino (www.finnkino.fi/eng) website.

The Art Deco **Cinema Orion** (Eerikinkatu 15, tel: 02 9533 8131; https://kavi.fi) at the national audiovisual archive shows classic Finnish and foreign arthouse films.

BARS AND NIGHTCLUBS

Most of the city's nightlife is centred in the area around the Central Railway Station. The party tends to start late: it's common for people to have a few drinks at home before hitting the town from 11pm onwards. Bars can stay open until 2am, nightclubs until 4am. The official drinking age is 18 and over but some clubs have a minimum age limit of 21 or 24. Entrance fees are anything from free to outrageous.

Designed by Alvar Aalto, the elegant **Ateljee Bar** (Yrjönkatu 26; tel. 20 123 4604 www.raflaamo.fi) on the 14th floor of the Sokos Torni Hotel is a fabulous place to sip a glass of champagne and contemplate the high life, with spectacular views that extend over the city and beyond.

After the auction houses and investment banks close for the day, their employees head to the opulent, chandeliered **Kämp Bar and Club** (Pohjoisesplanadi 29; www.hotelkamp.fi) for post-work cocktails and a wide selection of European wines. Another sophisticated choice is the **A21 Cocktail Lounge** (Annankatu 21; http://a21.fi) – you'll need to get dressed up and ring the doorbell for admittance to this sleek,

Mixing drinks at A21 Cocktail Lounge

chic, prize-winning place, which serves some peculiarly Finnish creations, infused with birch bark, rhubarb and sea buckthorn, alongside the classics.

For quirky Finnishness, head for Eerinkatu, where you'll find a clutch of charismatic bars originally founded by the film director Kaurismäki brothers. The **Andorra** (Eerinkatu 11; http://andorra.fi) complex comprises **Corona**, which attracts a young, hip crowd who come to talk, drink beer and play pool; **Dubrovnik Lounge and Lobby**, a live music venue; and **Kafe Moskva**, a small, "Brezhnevian-style" bar offering drinkers "a genuine soviet experience".

Bar Bäkkäri (Pohjoinen Rautatiekatu 21; www.bakkari.fi), former recipient of Helsinki's best bar accolade, is a real rock bar with a great atmosphere: bands playing upstairs at the weekend often join the partying crowds afterwards, and frequent theme nights keep the guests amused.

For a laidback, international crowd, seek out the great Irish bar **Molly Malone's** (Kaisaniemenkatu 1C; tel. 020 719 1970; www. mollymalones.fi), just a few metres from the central train station, which comes to life each night with live music performances.

Several Helsinki bars are famous for their summer terraces, where people flock to enjoy the warm bright nights. One such place is the well-to-do **Elite** (Etläinen Hesperiankatu 22; tel. 09 6128 5200; www.royalravintolat.com), filled with Art Deco flair. A few minutes' walk from the National Museum, this Helsinki institution was big amongst local artists back in its heyday. **LeBonk** (Yrjönkatu 24; tel. 044 981 1919; http://lebonk.fi), a large lounge-bar-cum-nightclub, was designed by eccentric Finnish artist Alvar Gullichsen, whose works are on display. Its rooftop terrace is a fashionable place to see and be seen when

☉ THE GAY SCENE

Helsinki is a tolerant, open city where LGBT visitors should feel at ease. Helsinki Pride (http://helsinkipride.fi) takes place over a week in late June, culminating in a parade that attracts around 8,000 participants.

As far as socialising goes, **Bar Loose** (Annankatu 21; www. barloose.com), while not specifically a gay bar, sells itself as "a liberal living room for good people", and is welcoming to all. An unmissable Finnish institution is **DTM** (Mannerheimintie 6 B; www.dtm.fi). "Don't Tell Mama", the largest gay bar/club in northern Europe, offers its patrons everything imaginable: from a daytime coffee bar to bingo to karaoke to a full-on nightclub with two dancefloors. Another upbeat club is **Hercules** (Pohjoinen Rautatiekatu 21; http://hercules. fi), which attracts a mostly male, over-30s crowd.

the weather warms. A little distance from the city centre in the green surroundings of Kaivopuisto Park is the legendary summer restaurant **Kaivohuone** (Iso Puistotie 1, Kaivopuisto Park; open May–Aug; http://helsinginkaivohuone. fi), also a late-night party joint that attracts the young and beautiful.

The roof terrace at LeBonk

Nightclubs often feature themed evenings and live music; for example the university-owned, rock-focused **Tavastia** (Urho Kekkosen katu 4–6; www.tavastiaklubi. fi); **The Circus** (Salomonkatu 1–3; www.thecircus.fi); and the long-standing **Kaarle XII** (Kasarmikatu 40; www.kaarle.fi), which is the place to be on Thursday nights.

SHOPPING

The main shopping district in Helsinki fits neatly into a rectangular area between the Central Railway Station, the Esplanadi, Mannerheimintie and Senate Square and the Market Hall. The two largest department stores and a shopping centre, connected by a tunnel, are to the east along Mannerheimintie, near the station.

Aleksanterinkatu and the smaller streets that cross it on a north–south axis contain some wonderful speciality shops: the "Tori Quarter", between Senate Square and Market Square, is full of design boutiques and chic cafés. The leading

Iittala glassware

Finnish design brands have flagship stores on Esplanadi, as do many large international brands. East of the cathedral, the Kruununhaka district is good for antiques.

Design District Helsinki (www.designdistrict.fi) is a marketing concept used to publicise the city's art museums, galleries and cutting-edge designers. A handy map, available in the tourist office, shows the location of around 100 boutiques selling clothing, jewellery and quintessentially Finnish homeware, located mainly in the Kamppi and Punavuori areas, a short walk southwest of the railway station.

The Finns have a flair for modernist design: the clean, functional lines that have influenced architecture and furniture throughout the world also turn up in locally made jewellery, clothing, glass and homeware. The Design Museum (see page 50) is a great place to bone up, with 75,000 Finnish-designed objects in its collection.

CERAMICS AND GLASSWARE

Arabia Factory Outlet (Hämeentie 135; tel: 0204 3910; www. arabia.fi) is the largest outlet for Arabia ceramics, Iittala glass, and Hackman and Pentik homeware. The factory, about 25 minutes' tram ride from downtown Helsinki, has a small museum upstairs, and first- and second-quality goods on sale downstairs. Guided factory tours are available on request (tel: 0204 39 5326; email: arabia.visitors@fiskars.com).

CLOTHING AND TEXTILES

Joutsen (Museokatu 8; tel: 020 749 5216; www.joutsen.com), the northernmost manufacturer of down products in the world, uses goose- and duck-down from the Arctic region to fill its toasty-warm products. These include everything from duvets and pil-lows to cosy slippers to an innovative range of coats and jackets.

Marimekko (Mikonkatu 1; tel: 050 572 5632; www.marimekko. fi) is the quintessential Finnish clothing designer, selling bold, brightly coloured items for men, women and children, as well as textiles for home use. The Hattroniemi outlet organises guided tours in the printing factory on request at tehtaanm yymala@marimekko.com.

Samuji (Erottajankatu 9 B (courtyard); tel: 040 350 7976; www. samuji.com) offers simple, stylish women's and men's clothing lines, created by some of Finland's best independent design-ers, with clean lines and a strong minimalist influence.

DEPARTMENT STORES

Stockmann (Aleksanterinkatu 52B; tel: 091 211; www.stock mann.fi), dating back to 1862, is the king of department stores, a seven-floor, city-block-hogging, age-old institution. You'll find plenty of high-quality Finnish merchandise here, and an excellent souvenir department. The connected Academic

Bookstore (Akateeminen Kirjakauppa), designed by Aalto, is spread over four floors.

Sokos (Mannerheimintie 9; tel: 010 766 5100; www.sokos.fi) is a smaller department store, based in an emblematic building that opened in 1952 for the Olympic Games.

FINNISH SPECIALITIES

Moomin Shop (Mannerheimintie 20 and at Helsinki-Vantaa Airport; tel: 040 192 0720; www.moominshop.fi), a small but perfectly stocked outlet on the 2nd floor of the Forum shopping centre, will be heaven on earth for fans of Moomintroll, Snufkin and Little My.

Saunamarket (Unioninkatu 32; tel: 0452243015; www.sauna market.fi) is the place to stock up on all your sauna essentials, such as sauna hats, bathrobes, birch whisks, skin-care products and sauna snacks.

JEWELLERY

Kalevala Koru (Pohjoisesplanadi 25-7, and at the Airport Shop at Helsinki Airport; tel: 0207 611 390; www.kalevala koru.com) is a fascinating jewellery store created in 1925 and owned entirely by a 4000-strong women's association. The Kalevala range is inspired by the Finnish epic poem, with pieces rendered in gold, silver and bronze. The store also sells silver Lapponia jewellery, once worn by Princess Leia in *Star Wars*. Both jewellery lines make occasional use of spectrolite, an unusual mineral in iridescent shades of green, dark blue and yellow.

MARKETS AND FLEA MARKETS

Helsinki's markets are full of colour and atmosphere and definitely worth a browse. **Kauppatori**, near the south harbour, is the main Helsinki market, and offers some attractive souvenirs, dolls, and leather and fur items on its stalls. The nearby Old Market Hall has an exceptional selection of delicatessen foods including unusual delicacies like bear meat. If you're shopping in the "Design District", pop into **Hietalahti Market Hall** for snacks or a sit-down meal. Outside in summer, the **Hietalahti Flea Market** sprawls across the market square. On one day in May and in August, the city has a **Cleaning Day** (**Siivouspäivä**), where everyone can bring unwanted goods out and sell them on the streets.

SHOPPING CENTRES

Forum (Mannerheimintie 20A; www.forum.fi) is the largest shopping centre in central Helsinki with 120 shops. The lower level contains a food hall and a choice of restaurants. **Kamppi** (Urho Kekkosenkatu 1; www.kamppi.fi) contains over one hundred retail stores, restaurants and supermarkets, while the basement holds the city's long-distance bus terminal.

SPORTS & ACTIVITIES

SAUNAS

A vital part of Finnish culture is the ubiquitous

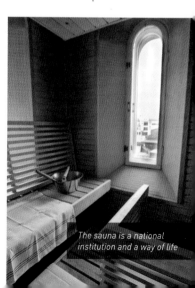

The sauna is a national institution and a way of life

sauna. Historically, the sauna was where women gave birth and bodies were laid out after death, and for most Finnish people the sauna experience is still a serious, sometimes spiritual, one. Saunas are usually segregated between the sexes. The natural wood-burning types are the most highly valued: the beautifully peaceful **Kulttuurisauna** (Wed–Sun 4pm–9pm; charge; www.kulttuurisauna.fi) in the Merihaka district is a new spin on this ancient tradition.

Today, most people have saunas in their homes, but three older public saunas remain northeast of the city centre in the Kallio/Sörnäinen districts. Entry costs between €10 and €14. Towels can be rented, and snacks are available:

Kotiharjun (Tue–Sun 2pm–8pm; charge; www.kotiharjun sauna.fi), at Harjutorinkatu 1, is another wood-burning sauna, dating back to 1928.

Löyly Sauna (Mon 4–10pm, Tue–Thur 1–10pm, Fri–Sat 1–11pm, Sun 1–10pm, morning sessions Thur and Sat 7.30–09.30am; charge; www.loylyhelsinki.fi), new in 2016 at Hernesaarenranta 4, is a stunning wood-clad venue that also has a restaurant with terrace overlooking the old harbour area.

Sauna Arla (Wed–Sun Fri 2/3pm–8/9.30pm, Sat–Sun from 2pm; charge; www.arlansauna.net), opened a year after Kotiharjun, is a near neighbour at Kaarlenkatu 15.

Sauna Hermanni (Mon–Fri 3pm–8pm, Sat 2pm–6pm; charge; www.saunahermanni.fi), at Hämeentie 63, has a 1950s vibe.

NATIONAL PARKS

Roaming forests and fells is an extremely popular pastime all over the country, encouraged by the legal concept of everyman's right, which allows wide-ranging access to the countryside. Finland has 38 national parks, managed by Metsähallitus (P.O. Box 94, Vernissakatu 4, FI-01301 Vantaa, tel: 0206 39 4000,

www.nationalparks.fi).
Sipoonkorpi and **Nuuksio**
(see page 72) national
parks are just 20km
and 35km from Helsinki
respectively, and easily
accessed by public trans-
port. Their visitor centres
can provide further information about hiking, ski-
ing, snow-shoe walking,
trail running, canoeing,
mushroom picking and
guided nature walks.

Nuuksio National Park

Finland is also a fine
place for **bird-watching**:
many migratory birds stop here before their yearly mass
migrations. For more information, visit Bird Life Finland (www.
birdlife.fi).

WATER ACTIVITIES

The country's wiggling shoreline provides visitors with excellent paddling opportunities. Natura Viva (00 358 10 292 4030;
http://kauppa.naturaviva.fi) has three-hour guided **sea kayaking** tours into the Helsinki archipelago.

Hietaniemi Beach (known to locals as 'Hietsu') is Helsinki's
biggest family beach, with a gently sloping swimming area
manned by lifeguards between June and mid-August. Take bus
55A from Kamppi. In summer, Helsinki's citizens also flock to the
recreational **Pihlajasaari Island**, with sandy beaches (including
a naturist beach) and sauna. The island can be reached by ferry
from Merisatama harbour between mid-May and August.

Linnanmäki Amusement Park

SPECTATOR SPORTS

The main spectator sport is **ice hockey**, a major Finnish passion. The season runs from September to April. IFK Helsinki plays home matches at the Helsinki Ice Hall (Helsingin Jäähalli), just north of the Olympic Stadium; while Jokerit play at the Hartwall Arena.

ACTIVITIES FOR CHILDREN

Family attractions in Helsinki include the **Korkeasaari Zoo** (see page 68), **Linnanmäki Amusement Park** (see page 59), and a small aquarium, **Sea Life Helsinki** (tel: 09-565 8200; www.sealife.fi), with displays from the tropics to the Baltic and a walk-through underwater glass tunnel. On the third floor of the National Museum (see page 43), **Workshop Vintti** (Tue–Sun noon–4pm) is an interactive exploration of Finland's history – kids can build a log house, harness a horse, weave a rug and sit on an emperor's throne!

Just a 15-minute train ride from downtown Helsinki, **Heureka** (tel: 09 8579 288; www.heureka.fi), the Finnish Science Centre in Vantaa-Tikkurila, has a range of "hands-on" exhibitions, a planetarium and some basketball-playing rats.

Serena Water Park (tel: 09-887 0550; www.serena.fi) in Espoo can easily be reached by bus from Helsinki and is open year-round.

CALENDAR OF EVENTS

Early Jan Lux Helsinki (www.luxhelsinki.fi) Art installations created using light illuminate the city.

Feb Musica Nova (http://musicanova.fi) Week-long music festival, held in alternate years; Parade of Graduating Students along Esplanadi.

Good Friday Via Crucis. Passion-play procession from Kaisaniemi Park to Senate Square.

Easter Saturday Easter Bonfires. Bonfires on Seurasaari Island scare away witches, who traditionally wreak havoc today.

April Jazz Espoo: (www.apriljazz.fi) Helsinki's largest jazz event, in Espoo.

1 May May Day. Traditional parades and a huge picnic in Kaivopuisto Park.

May Lovely Helsinki. The city is decorated with flowers to celebrate spring; Cirko Festival (www.cirko.fi/en) The best of contemporary circus; World Village Festival (www.maailmakylassa.fi/english) Free family festival with a multicultural focus – music, dancing and food.

Mid June: Taste of Helsinki (www.tasteofhelsinki.fi) Four-day culinary festival.

12 June Helsinki Day (www.helsinkipaiva.fi/en) Happy Birthday, Helsinki! Fun-filled celebration to mark the city's founding in 1550.

21 June Midsummer's Eve. Traditional bonfires, folk dancing and midsummer enchantment on Seurasaari Island.

End June Tuska Open-Air Metal Festival (www.tuska-festival.fi) Biggest heavy-metal festival in Northern Europe, held at Suvilahti power plant.

Mid Aug Helsinki Festival (www.helsinginjuhlaviikot.fi) Finland's biggest cultural festival: two weeks packed with music, film, art and theatre; Helsinki City Marathon (www.helsinkicitymarathon.fi); Flow Festival (www.flowfestival.com) Urban music and culture at Suvilahti power plant.

Early Sept Helsinki Design Week (www.helsinkidesignweek.com) Largest design event in Northern Europe, with exhibitions, shows and workshops.

Early Oct Helsinki Baltic Herring Fair. Fishermen sell herring and other archipelago products from their boats at Market Square.

Dec St Thomas Christmas Market in Esplanadi Park.

6 Dec Finnish Independence Day celebrations.

31 Dec New Year's Eve. Music, singing and fireworks in Senate Square.

EATING OUT

FOOD HISTORY

Unlike other parts of Europe, Finland never had a strong bourgeoisie with the wealth and leisure to develop rich culinary traditions. The country's food history is a tale of austerity. Finland's isolated rural economy and unforgiving climate, with short summers and long winters, meant that harvested food had to last for six or more months. Finns depended on dried, smoked and pickled meats and fish dishes that would keep for several seasons.

Luckily for visitors, the situation today is different. Modern menus have been heavily influenced by the New Nordic Kitchen movement, which arose in Denmark in 2004. The movement advocates using local, organic and sustainable products, and has seen the Nordic countries, including Finland, develop a fresh pride and enthusiasm for ingredients that are unique to the region. There is also a sense of playfulness, as old-style "grandmother's" recipes are revisited and revitalised to suit modern tastes.

Finland was fought over for centuries by its Swedish and Russian neighbours, and both countries have had a heavy influence on its cuisine. Stroganoff, hotpots, squidgy black bread, blinis, sauerkraut and pasties such as the rice-stuffed *karjalanpiirakat* hail from Russia; while meatball dishes, hard cheeses, and a startling selection of pickled herring are some of Sweden's gifts. The Swedish *smörgåsbord* has also found its way to Finland, where it is known as *seisova pöytä*. A few Helsinki restaurants also have Sámi-influenced menus, showcasing Arctic specialities such as reindeer and bear.

WHERE TO EAT

Helsinki has a wide selection of eating places, ranging from four Michelin-starred restaurants (Ask at Vironkatu 8; Chef & Sommelier at Huvilakatu 28; Demo at Uudenmaankatu 9–11; Olo at Pohjoisesplanadi 5) to streetside kiosks selling grilled food. Most of the city's restaurants produce food to a high standard, and have menus that change with the seasons: look for crayfish in July, chanterelles in August, Baltic herring in September, and goose, moose and reindeer in the autumn hunting season. There are also an increasing number of restaurants serving cuisine from other cultures, with classy Japanese, Chinese, Lebanese, Indian and Latin American options available.

As in other Nordic countries, where long winter days make summer sunshine all the more precious, outdoor cafés and bars are popular in the warmer months. It's a rare pleasure to sit on a green terrace, savouring a light lunch and watching the crowds pass by. Cafés are also the place to participate in a vital Finnish ritual, the consumption of coffee and *pulla*, sweet buns flavoured with cardamom.

Outdoor cafés are popular in summer

Foodies should visit the city's markets. In summer, stalls on the market squares overflow with seasonal fruit and veg. In winter time, head inside: the indoor market halls can provide you with fresh fish, meat and game, as well as delicatessen-style nibbles.

The Abattoir (Teurastamo), in the Sörnäinen district north-east of the centre, has become a foodie paradise with several restaurants, an ice-cream factory and a "flavour laboratory", and events such as a monthly farmers' market, a night market and the summertime "Street Food Thursday".

FINNISH CUISINE

Fish

Fish has always been important in the Finnish diet – unsurprising, considering the country's myriad lakes and rivers and long, long coastline. Bream, burbot, perch and pike are traditional species, and salmon are omnipresent. What isn't available locally can be readily imported from neighbouring countries such as Norway.

☉ TASTES FROM THE TREES

Finland's whispering forests have added extra flavour to the nation's food. Edible substances have been found in all three of the country's most common trees. Birch gives Xylitol, a sweetener very kind to teeth; spruce spring shoots are used to make sweet jam, a delicacy served with desserts; and pine is a good source of tar, extracted from the tree in traditional tar-burning pits. The light tar has a soothing aroma, and is used in Finnish sweets and ice cream. Pine is also raw material for the Finnish-invented Benecol, a margarine-style spread that has been found to have cholesterol-lowering qualities.

Fresh seafood toasts

Smoked fish is a speciality, although it may also be grilled, glow-fired, steamed, or basted in the oven.

Salmon soup (*lohikeitto*) is another subtle delicacy: only a pinch of salt is added to the liquid, but the main taste comes from the fish. Each way of cooking salmon in Finland gives a distinctive experience, but *graavi lohi* (raw salmon marinated for a day in salt and herbs) is delicious. *Graavi* is the Finnish version of *sushi* – but instead of rice and seaweed, it is served with small potatoes and dill.

While Finnish salmon should not be missed, don't forget to try *siika* as well. This white fish has a more subtle taste, and is also best in the *graavi* variety, with potatoes and dill. Tiny vendace (*muikku*), sometimes served with garlic and cream, are an ever-popular Finnish snack: this unpretentious little fish has more taste than all tropical varieties combined. Lamprey, a strange, jawless fish found in the rivers of western Finland, is another fine experience of Finnish haute cuisine. It is nearly always charcoal-grilled and eaten whole.

Meat and game

Much of Finland's tasty elk meat disappears into private freezers during the hunting season, but semi-domesticated reindeer is more common. The Lapland speciality is *poronkäristys* (reindeer casserole), served with mashed potatoes and cranberry (lingonberry). The best part of reindeer is fillet steak, but a real delicacy is smoked reindeer heart, with a cedar aroma and a subtle taste. You can find this latter dish on the menu at Juuri (see page 114). The best restaurants in Finland also serve game birds in season (late summer/autumn), with wild duck being most common.

Sausage (*makkara*) is very popular in summer – best grilled with local mustard. It also appears in the traditional Finnish soul food dish *pyttipannu*, a hash of fried potato, sausage and onions, topped with fried eggs. Meatballs (*lihapullat*) are another sturdy staple deriving from Sweden.

Vegetables, fruit and grains

Rye bread (*ruisleipä*) is king in Finland, and served at every meal. It has an amazing ability to resist spoiling: in Finland's agrarian past,

Tinned reindeer meat

farmhouses had an annual baking day, and the resulting rye bread was then eaten over the course of the year. Common forms include leavened crispbread (*näkkileipä*), dried into thin slices; and the stickier, harder *jälkiuunileipä*, delicious with cheese and cold milk.

Barley is a traditional staple, which some restaurants are reintroducing to replace rice and pasta (which are common in Finland too). Barley, oats, rye and rice are all used for porridges, typical breakfast items in Finnish homes.

Potatoes are available all year round, but their most delicious incarnation is as the tiny, nutty new potatoes that come into season in July.

Root vegetables and brassicas traditionally kept Finns going through the winter. Swede, turnip and cabbage are seldom considered "gourmet food", but some restaurants such as Restaurant Aino (see page 111) make a virtue of them in dishes such as beef and barley-filled cabbage rolls (*kaalikääryleet*), served with mashed potatoes and lingonberry jam.

One special element in Finnish cuisine is the abundance of wild berries, fungi and herbs, gathered from the forests. Blueberries and sweet, wild strawberries are readily available in July, the native sour cranberries (lingonberries) by September. Out of 2,000 varieties of Finnish fungi, around 500 are edible – many varieties turn up in restaurants and on market stalls in August and September.

Vegetarians

Even as recently as 10 years ago, vegetarians were met with bafflement. Today there are several restaurants in the city that serve only vegetarian, vegan and gluten-free fare. Most other Helsinki restaurants have at least one vegetarian option on the menu.

Sweet treats

Berries are often used to create juicy desserts, such as blueberry pie, tart-tasting lingonberry pie, strawberry cake and the delightfully named *lakkakakku* (cloudberry cake).

Stodgier fare includes doughnuts and cinnamon buns, usually eaten with morning coffee. For a love-it-or-hate-it snack, look out for salt liquorice in supermarkets.

Speciality food

Finland is a large country, and all kinds of regional delicacies have evolved over the years. Many make their way to Helsinki: look out for Tampere's *mustamakkara* ("black sausage"), which contains spices, barley and blood in real gut; delicious Karelian pasties, filled with buttery rice; the strange, "squeaky" cheese *leipäjuusto*, from the northwest coast, often eaten with yellow cloudberries; and bear meat and reindeer stew (*poronkäristys*) from Lapland.

Christmas food in Finland is very traditional, and still very much loved, in spite of being rather simple by today's standards. Little has changed on the festive menu over the past century: ham, salmon, casseroles and dried codfish always feature, and there are plenty of desserts, including ginger biscuits and the popular star-shaped plum tart, *joulutorttu*. At Easter, Finns consume *mämmi* (a malt-based pudding) and drink *sima* (mead), while *tippaleipä* pastries are the May Day speciality. Festival times apart, Finnish food varies both seasonally and geographically, making it an endless source of fascination and providing pleasant surprises for visitors to the country.

Meal times

Meal times are early compared to some European cities – usually 6.30am–10am for breakfast, 11am–1pm for lunch and 6.30–9pm for dinner. Inexpensive lunches (*lounas*) can be had at cafés (*kahvilat*). Note that restaurants may close on Sunday and/or Monday, and many shut completely for the month of July.

WHAT TO DRINK

Medium-strength beer is available at most cafés, and a full range of beverages is sold at fully licensed restaurants and bars. Restaurants serve beer from 9am and other alcoholic drinks from 11am, but stop serving them half an hour before they close. The basic measures are 4cl (1.3fl oz) for spirits, 8cl (2.7fl oz) for fortified wines and 12cl (4fl oz) for table wines; beer is served either in 0.33-litre (0.7 pint) bottles or in 0.4-litre (0.8 pint) glasses. Not all restaurants are licensed, so check before you go. The minimum legal age for drinking alcohol in restaurants is 18.

Beer is ubiquitous, and one of the "big five" is most usually served: Koff, Lapin

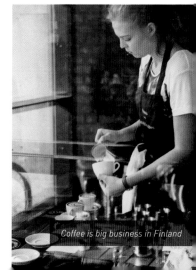
Coffee is big business in Finland

Kulta, Karhu, Karjala or Olvi (this last is in fact the only major brewery still Finnish-owned). Most beer is usually 4.5 or 5.2 percent, stronger brews can reach 7 percent.

Wine, relatively expensive, is often drunk with meals, and you will find both local and imported vintages on offer. There are now around 40 wineries in Finland. Strawberries, blackcurrants and redcurrants, among others, are used to produce a distinctive red wine – not exactly Burgundy, but it is a well-balanced berry drink with 12 percent strength.

Vodka is particularly popular in Finland and Finlandia is the country's best-selling brand, distilled with crystal-clear water that has been naturally filtered through deep moraine ridges. Berries grow everywhere and the Finns use them to make liqueurs, such as Lapponia Lakka, which is made from cloudberries.

The sale of alcohol is strictly controlled in Finland; strong beer (over 4.7 percent), spirits and wine can be bought only from Alko (the state alcohol monopoly); Stockmann's department store in Helsinki has an Alko unit on the ground floor. Medium- and lower-alcohol beer can be bought in supermarkets.

TO HELP YOU ORDER...

A table, please **Pöytä, kiitos.**
We would like to order... **Haluaisimme tilata...**
What do you recommend? **Mitä te suosittelette?**
Enjoy your meal! **Hyvää ruokahalua!**
Could I have the bill, please? **Saisko laskun, kiitos?**

Beer **olut**	fruit **hedelmät**
bread **leipä**	ice cream **jäätelö**
butter **voi**	meat **liha**
coffee **kahvi**	menu **ruokalista**
dessert **jälkiruoka**	milk **maito**
fish **kala**	pepper **pippuri**

potatoes **perunoita**
rice **riisi**
salad **salaatti**
salt **suola**
sandwich **voileipä**

soup **soppa**
sugar **sokeri**
tea **tee**
water **juomavesi**
wine **viini**

...AND READ THE MENU

ankerias eel
grillattua grilled
hampurilainen hamburger
hauki pike
hernekeitto pea soup
hirvenliha elk
juusto cheese
kakku cake
kalamurekepihvit fishcake
kana chicken
karjalan piirakka Karelian pasty
kinkku ham
kirjolohi rainbow trout
lammas lamb
lihapullat meatballs
lohi salmon
makkara salami
mansikka strawberry
mäti fish roe
merenelävät seafood
muikku vendace
muna egg
muurain arctic cloudberry
mustaherukka blackcurrant

nakki hotdog
naudanliha beef
omena apple
palapihvi beef casserole
perunoita potatoes
pihvi steak
porkkana carrot
poronliha reindeer
pulla bun
puolukka lingonberry
puuro porridge
rautu arctic char
ruisleipä dark rye bread
savusilli smoked herring
sianliha pork
sieni mushroom
siiki whitefish
silakka Baltic herring
simpukka mussel
sinappi mustard
suklaa chocolate
turska cod
vaapukka raspberry
vasikanliha veal
vihannekset vegetables

PLACES TO EAT

We have used the following symbols to give an idea of the average cost of a three-course meal without wine:

€€€ over €60
€€ €35 to 60
€ below €35

RAUTATIENTORI

Pääposti €€ *Mannerheiminaukio 1B, tel: 020 729 6712*, www.fazer.fi/paaposti. This lunch restaurant, set in the main post office building next to the railway station, does a grand selection of traditional Finnish dishes, priced at a reasonable €10 (€2 extra for dessert).

Raffaello €€ *Aleksanterinkatu 46, tel: 010 76 64700*, www.raflaamo.fi/fi/helsinki/raffaello. A Mediterranean restaurant perfect for a relaxing lunch buffet (€12), though there are pricier à la carte dishes, such as grilled salmon or seafood linguini, available as well.

Venn €€ *Mikonkatu 4, tel: 010 76 64672*, www.raflaamo.fi/fi/helsinki/venn-helsinki. Recently taken over by Raflaamo, this cheerful, busy spot is a restaurant/bar right off Esplanadi. Great burgers and steaks.

Virgin Oil Company € *Mannerheimintie 5, tel: 010-766 4000*; www.virginoil.fi. Located just around the corner from the railway station in the old student house, this American-style restaurant serves a vast selection of pizza and pasta dishes. There is a concert venue just upstairs, so it can get very busy on weekend evenings.

Vltava €€ *Elielinaukio 2, tel: 010-766 3650*, www.raflaamo.fi/en/helsinki/vltava. Ideally situated just next to the railway station, this Czech restaurant serves thick *wursts* and traditional sausages. They're also renowned for their beer selection, culled straight from the best areas of the Czech Republic.

MARKET SQUARE AND ESPLANADI

Aino €€ *Pohjoisesplanadi 21, tel: 09 624 327,* www.ravintolaaino.fi. The Aino has a fine location by the Esplanadi and a relaxing atmosphere. The menu, which changes seasonally, includes Finnish fresh- and salt-water fish, lamb, reindeer, root vegetables, wild mushrooms and berries. Don't forget to try 'Aino's snaps', the restaurant's own version of schnapps, which is served in handmade stoneware cups.

Esplanad € *Pohjoisesplanadi 37, tel: 09 665 496,* www.esplanad.fi. This classic establishment doesn't have the best decor, but in terms of central city cafés, there isn't that much that can beat it for location. In addition to the great fresh-brewed coffee, there are sandwiches, soups and snacks. Best for coffee and cakes, consumed at a sunny outdoor seat.

Haven €€€ *Eteläranta 16, tel: 09 6824 2840;* www.hotelhaven.fi.This restaurant, next to Market Square, is inside a 19th-century Empire-style building designed by Engel. The building and decor are traditional and the cuisine, although traditional, has a modern twist. Try their brew dinner: a three-meal course accompanied by a beer tasting.

Kappeli €€ *Esplanadi Park, tel: 010 766 3880,* www.kappeli.fi. This classic, grand house – forged out of glass and iron – dates back to 1867. It looks right onto the Esplanadi and is perhaps the most popular place for people to come and unwind. Lots of live entertainment both inside and out during the summer. Classic Finnish dishes, from light open sandwiches to mains of reindeer and salmon.

Kuurna €€ *Meritullinkatu 6, tel: 010-281 8241,* www.kuurna.com. This tiny, bohemian restaurant offers traditional home-style meals that are given a contemporary twist. Typical dishes might include poached pike perch and beef roast, served with polenta and salsa verde. The short but considered menu changes fornightly. Two sittings, from 6pm to 8pm, and from 8.30pm.

MS Katharina € *Kauppatori.* Moored just next to the Market Hall in the winter, this wooden passenger ship is an extremely cosy place to come for a coffee or hot chocolate on a chilly afternoon. The café is fixed into the galley of the boat, and they also serve baguettes and soup.

Toca €€€ *Unioninkatu 18, tel: 04 4237 9922*, www.toca.fi. Modern Finnish cuisine with an Italian twist served up in an industrial setting. Good wine list.

KATAJANOKKA

Bellevue €€€ *Rahapajankatu 3, tel: 09 179 560*, http://restaurant bellevue.com. In the shadow of the Uspenski Orthodox Cathedral this is the oldest Russian restaurant in Helsinki, opened in 1917. The ambience is delightfully old-fashioned and the cuisine traditional – especially *blinis* at the beginning of Lent and at the Easter feasts. Serves bear in sausage form, and as steak (€39) served with boletus mushrooms.

Nokka €€–€€€ *Kanavaranta 7 F, tel: 09 6128 5600*, www.ravintola nokka.fi. Located in one of the old red-brick buildings under the Orthodox Cathedral, this is a restaurant of great character with exposed brick walls, wooden beams and an eclectic decor featuring, among other things, old divers' helmets as light fittings. The menu features Arctic char, duck, lamb, snails and wild mushrooms, with wild berries for puddings.

Sipuli €€€ *Kanavaranta 7, tel: 09 6128 5500*, www.ravintolasipuli.fi. This formal and expensive Franco-Finnish restaurant is set in the same restored warehouse as Nokka. The small, rich gastro dishes here (roasted spring chicken and pomegranate with vermouth froth, or poached Arctic char with shellfish paella and dark citrus sauce, for example) can be paired with wines from its extensive list.

MANNERHEIMINTIE

Ateljé Finne €€€ *Arkadiankatu 14, tel: 010 281 8242*, www.ateljefinne.fi. This intimate little spot was once the studio of sculptor Gunnar Finne, and it maintains an arty atmosphere and clientele. Traditional Finnish dishes are given a modern bistro twist – don't leave without trying the liquorice-spiced crème brûlée.

Elite €€ *Eteläinen Hesperiankatu 22, tel: 09 6128 5200*, www.elite.fi. A restaurant classic from the 1930s, traditionally favoured by Finland's cultural and artistic circles. The international menu also includes some Finnish classics like fried Baltic herrings with mashed potatoes and sirloin steak with creamed onion à la Tauno Palo, who was one of the most popular actors in Finland from the 1930s to the 1960s. There is also a green outdoor terrace.

Farang €€–€€€ *Ainonkatu 3, tel: 010-322 9385*, http://farang.fi. Hands down Helsinki's best Asian restaurant, this winner infuses fresh ingredients with finely balanced flavours. Its fusion food is innovative without being pretentious – and veggies can delight in a tasting menu of their very own. Based in the lovely setting of Kunsthalle Helsinki.

Kuu €€ *Töölönkatu 27, tel: 09 2709 0973*, www.ravintolakuu.fi. This relaxed bistro is handy for pre-opera dining – the Opera House is just 300m/yards away. "The Moon" serves Finnish classics and related Scandinavian fare, such as smoked salmon roe, whitefish with fennel sauce, or reindeer steaks.

Lasipalatsi €€ *Mannerheimintie 22–24, tel: 09 7424 290*, www.ravintola lasipalatsi.fi. Between the railway station and the bus station, this restaurant is located in the functionalist "Glass Palace", and has 1930s-style decor in keeping with the building. The menu, like the seasons, changes four times a year and features typical Finnish ingredients such as fresh fish, local cheeses and full-flavoured wild berries.

Lehtovaara €€–€€€ *Mechelininkatu 39, tel: 09 440 833*, www. lehtovaara.fi. Established in 1940 in a great spot by Sibelius Park, this is one of Helsinki's longest-standing restaurants and an excellent place to catch a bit of Old Finland. The Finnish meals are best enjoyed in the glass winter-garden terrace. The wine list has over 100 vintages, and those with a sweet tooth will delight in the restaurant's dessert buffet.

THE "DESIGN DISTRICT"

Café Bar No 9 € *Uudenmaankatu 9, tel: 09 621 4059*, http://bar9.net. A few minutes' walk away from the Swedish Theatre, at the head of the Esplanadi, this relaxed little café/bar is popular with a younger, student crowd. The single-page menu offers a surprisingly wide variety of sandwiches, salads, soups, stir-fried dishes and pasta, all at very economical prices.

Corso €€ *Korkeavuorenkatu 45, tel: 09 666 116*, http://corsodining.fi. Formerly known as Gastone, Corso offers a lighter version of the Italian classics Gastone was famed for. Save space for the cheese platter; the staff can recommend a wine to go with it.

Ekberg € *Bulevardi 9, tel: 09 6811 860*, www.ekberg.fi. Set just off the main drag on quiet, quaint Bulevardi, this landmark café is over 150 years old, and has a palpably authentic turn of the century feel to it. Best for cakes, patisserie and freshly-baked loaves. It's also a good place for breakfast, opening at 7.30am with a buffet spread.

Juuri €€ *Korkeavuorenkatu 27, tel: 09-635 732*, http://juuri.fi. This unique, central restaurant serves excellent mains, but the prime delight lies in the choosing and chomping of *sapas*, or Finnish tapas. Juuri takes staple dishes from "grandmother's kitchen" and gives them a whole new spin, creating some of the most unusual dishes you'll ever try in Finland. An absolute must is the smoked reindeer heart.

Lappi €€ *Annankatu 22, tel: 645 550*, www.lappires.com. A typical Lapland-style restaurant with a cosy interior that is a re-creation of a traditional wooden summer house. The cuisine, too, is authentic. Starting with a Lappish aperitif, you might then try sirloin of reindeer with creamed juniper berry potatoes and game sauce, and round off your meal with delicious Lappish farm cheese in cinnamon cream.

Pastor Drink & Dine €€ *Erottajankatu 4, tel: 040 034 4700*, www.pastorrestaurant.fi. A cool, cozy place with a menu of fusion Peruvian and Japanese cuisines. Portions are on the small side. The cocktails are delicious and the venue turns into a nightclub at the weekend.

Ragu €€€ *Ludviginkatu 3-5, tel: 09 596 659,* www.ragu.fi. Ragu impresses. In addition to the à la carte menu, there are several tasting menus (including a vegetarian version) that focus on haute-fusion Scandinavian-style dishes with Italian elements. The flavour-packed dishes are complemented by a long Italian wine list.

Saaga €€ *Bulevardi 34, tel: 09-7425 5544,* www.ravintolasaaga.fi. There's something slightly kitsch in the décor (think birch bark, Shaman drums and antlers), but the Lappish food here is authentic. Try reindeer, Arctic char, salted fungi and exotic berries... or do you have the stomach for creamy bear soup?

Salve €€ *Hietalahdenranta 11, tel: 010-76 64280,* www.raflaamo.fi/fi/helsinki/salve. This restaurant-pub serves good traditional Finnish meals in a distinctly maritime atmosphere, and is particularly famous for its fried herring (though drinking is often a more popular reason to come here). Looks onto Helsinki's world-famous shipyards.

ULLANLINNA AND KAIVOPUISTO

Chef & Sommelier €€–€€€ *Huvilakatu 28, tel: 0400 959440,* http://chefetsommelier.fi. One of Helsinki's four Michelin-starred restaurants, Chef & Sommelier uses organic, fair-trade, local ingredients to create dishes that explode with flavour. The tasting menus come in every size from three to nine courses, and can be adapted for vegetarians if you notify the restaurant in advance.

Seahorse €€ *Kapteeninkatu 11, tel: 09 628 169,* www.seahorse.fi. This restaurant has entertained such celebs as Dizzy Gillespie and Pablo Neruda. Surprisingly, the menu is good value, even for the not-so-famous, and features some tasty Finnish classics such as herring, meatballs and perch à la Mannerheim.

KALLIO

Meripaviljonki *Meripaviljonki, Säästöpankinranta 3, tel: 020 7425 320,* www.ravintolameripaviljonki.fi. There was a huge buzz surrounding this beautiful floating glass restaurant when it opened in 2015 near Hakaniemi Market. The menu focuses on fresh fish dishes. Beautiful seaviews are a bonus.

Raiku € *Hämeentie 1, tel: 044 323 2515,* http://raiku.net. A stand-out lunch restaurant, this cheerful orange-painted place inside Hakaniemi Market Hall does simple soups, salads and hot mains to the highest standards. Everything is made from scratch on the premises, and there is always a veggie option.

SUOMENLINNA FORTRESS

Suomenlinnan Panimo €€ *Rantakasarmi, Suomenlinna C 1, tel: 020 7425 307,* www.panimoravintola.fi; *open year-round.* This is the best of Suomenlinna's sit-down restaurants, serving fresh fish and traditional meaty Finnish dishes, such as glazed pork, lamb sausages and roasted reindeer. The restaurant has its own microbrewery, concocting seasonal ales and the appropriately-named Tin Soldier cider, and has a lovely sunny garden in which to enjoy them. Located in the Jetty Barracks (Rantakasarmi) next to the HSL ferry harbour.

HELSINKI'S ISLANDS

NJK €€–€€€ *Valkosaari, tel: 09 6128 6500,* www.ravintolanjk.fi; *open May–Sept.* Several of Helsinki's islands contain nothing more than a seasonal restaurant. Valkosaari contains the Yacht Club's NJK, based in a turn-of-the-century villa. Summon the spirit of the Nordic summer by hopping aboard the tiny ferry (from Valkosaari pier, near Olympic terminal) and dining on crayfish, while admiring views over the water to Market Square. Ferry price included in restaurant bill.

A–Z TRAVEL TIPS

A SUMMARY OF PRACTICAL INFORMATION

A

ACCOMMODATION

Hotels in Finland have a well-deserved reputation for cleanliness, a wide range of facilities, good service and comfortable, albeit rather small, rooms, regardless of their price category. Official hotel ratings are not used in Finland, but the vast majority of hotels would be considered to be in the three- or four-star class. They do tend to be expensive for the facilities provided, although if you are patient, there are bargains to be had. Discounts are often available at weekends and in summer, when hotels lose their business and conference trade.

Most Helsinki options are international (Hilton, Radisson) or Finnish chain hotels, comfortable but unremarkable. Finnish chains include Best Western Finland (tel: 0800-12010, www.bestwestern.fi), Cumulus (tel: 09-73352, www.cumulus.fi), Finlandia Hotels (tel: 09 684 1440, www.finlandiahotels.fi), the Palace Kämp group (tel: 020 770 4705, www.kampgroup.fi), Scandic Hotels (tel: +46 8 517 517 20, www.scandic hotels.fi), Sokos Hotels (tel: 020 1234 600, www.sokoshotels.fi), and the budget Omena Hotels (tel: 0600 555 222, www.omenahotels.com), who keep costs low by not having reception staff.

Most Helsinki hotels are in the centre of town in an almost rectangular area between Central Railway Station in the north, Esplanadi in the south, Mannerheimintie to the west and Senate Square and Market Hall to the east. There are a couple of larger ones along Mannerheimintie, overlooking Töölönlahti Bay and near Hakaniemi Market.

Helsinki Expert has a hotel booking service at the railway station (tel: 09 2288 1600) and at the main tourist office (Pohjoisesplanadi 19; tel: 09 2288 1500).

For something more homey, Helsinki Bed and Breakfast (Vellamonkatu 12-14 B 32, tel: 050 5849054; http://en.hbb.fi) can fix you up with a comfortable B&B room or private apartment.

The website Visit Helsinki (www.visithelsinki.fi) keeps an up-to-date list of accommodation options.

AIRPORTS

Finland's main international airport, **Helsinki-Vantaa Airport** (www.helsinki-vantaa.fi), is a modern facility with an excellent range of services located about 20km (12 miles) north of Helsinki city centre. It is connected by the Finnair City Bus (€6.70) and local bus (€5) to Helsinki. Travel time is approximately 35 minutes. The Finnair bus stops at many of the major hotels on the way from the airport to the city centre, but only picks up at the central railway station and the Hesperia Park bus stop on the reverse route. The train to the city takes about 30 minutes; the route is serviced by two lines: I and P (€5). There is also a "shared" taxi stand at the airport. Expect to pay around €50 for a taxi to any destination in the city centre.

B

BICYCLE RENTAL

Bicycles are a practical and fun means of transport in Helsinki: the city has several hundred miles of well-maintained cycle paths. A good year-round hire shop is **Bicyclean Helsinki Katajanokka** (Luotsikatu 14; tel: 044 2915 331; May–Sept Mon noon–7pm, Tues–Sun 9am–7pm, Oct–Apr Mon noon–6pm, Tues–Fri 10am–6pm, Sat 10am–4pm; www.bicyclean helsinki.com). Prices start from €20 per day.

BUDGETING FOR YOUR TRIP

Flights to Finland vary according to departure airport, carrier and time of year, but you can expect to pay around €120 to €200 for a return London–Helsinki flight in July in economy class.

Compared to other countries in Europe, Finland is expensive. A dorm bed in a youth hostel costs around €20, while a hotel room is likely to cost upwards of €100 per night.

Many lunch places offer a good-value meal deal costing around €10, which usually includes a main course, plus salad or soup, bread and coffee. Otherwise, dining out is expensive. A three-course meal without wine at a mid-level restaurant costs around €50. Alcohol in a restaurant is equally pricey, with a 0.33 litre glass of beer costing around €7, and a small glass of wine from €8 upwards. Many bars and restaurants have a "wardrobe" charge of around €3, which you'll have to pay whether you have a coat on or not. Groceries tend to be around the EU average.

Museum entrance usually costs between €6 and €12.

Those on a budget can enjoy the city's unusual architecture, wandering streets such as the Art-Nouveau Luotsikatu, or visiting Kamppi Chapel of Silence or Helsinki Music Centre. Suomenlinna makes a cheap day trip – you can visit this extraordinary island for the price of a local-transport ticket (€5). Cheap places to eat include the coffee tents in Helsinki's market squares, while late at night you can find fairly inexpensive food (for example a €3 hamburger) at a *grilli* kiosk. Some museums offer free entry on a certain day of the month. Discounts for seniors and students are widely available.

C

CAMPING

Rastila Camping Helsinki (Karavaanikatu 4; tel: 09 310 78517; rastilacamping@hel.fi; open year-round) is a modern five-star campsite, with 80 tent and 165 caravan pitches, cabins and cottages for hire, and a summer family hostel. It's in Vuosaari, about 15km (9 miles) east of Helsinki centre, and is easily accessed from the Rastila Metro station. Booking ahead is strongly advised in summer.

Finland has some 330 campsites. For options elsewhere in the country, see the website of the Finnish Campingsite Association (Suomen Leirintäalueyhdistys; Tulppatie 14, FI-00880 Helsinki; tel: 09 4774 0740; www.camping.fi).

CAR HIRE

A car is not really necessary in Helsinki. The city centre is very walkable, and the public transport system is excellent.

If you do feel in need of a car, several international agencies have outlets at the airport, and also in the centre: Avis (Malminkatu 24; tel: 010 436 2222; www.avis.fi), Europcar (Elielinaukio 5; tel: 0403 062 803; www.europcar.fi), Hertz (Runeberginkatu 5; tel: 020 555 2300; www.hertz.com), Sixt (Hilton Hotel, John Stenbergin ranta 4; tel: 020-1122553; http://fi.sixt.com).

CLIMATE

Helsinki is actually quite mild considering its latitude. Although the North Atlantic brings cold air, the moderating influence of the warming Gulf Stream keeps the temperatures bearable. The city has four seasons. Summers are generally pleasant and mild – the brightest month is June, with 19 hours of sunlight, and the warmest is July, with an average temperature of 17.8°C (64.0°F). The air gets crisp and cold in September, as autumn approaches. Winters can be bitter: the coldest time is late January/early February, when temperatures can drop as low as –15°C (5°F) and the sea freezes over. After the chilly winter darkness, the coming of spring in April is a welcome relief.

CLOTHING

The weather in Helsinki is changeable – the best advice is to bring layers of clothing, regardless of the season. Finns tend to dress down, unless attending an important formal occasion. Generally you won't feel out of place anywhere in casual clothing.

Finland can get very hot in summer. Sun block and a sun hat are a must, as is a swimsuit for the many sandy beaches around the city. However, you can't always depend on temperate weather. Bring a raincoat, just in case; and a fleece or similar to keep off the cool evening air. Many of the city streets are cobbled, so it's a good idea to wear sturdy walking shoes.

Helsinki is famous for its bitter winters, when decent cold-weather outer clothing is a must. Again, though, layers are key – most Finnish buildings are very well heated in winter, so you'll want to be able to peel off once you get inside. Don't forget to bring heavy-duty, warm footwear (preferably boots) with a good grip, as roads and pavements can be icy.

CRIME AND SAFETY

Finland is one of the safest countries in Europe, and for the most part crime will not be an issue. Occasional pickpocketing has been known on the Helsinki metro and at the main railway station. Be alert in crowded places or when using cash machines, take common-sense precautions with valuables and you will be fine.

The police in Finland generally keep a low profile. If you need to report a crime, the police station is at Pasilanraitio 13, tel: 0295 470 011 (Mon–Fri 8am–4.15pm).

D

DISABLED TRAVELLERS

Finland has good legislation in place for disabled people, and all new buildings are legally required to have access in terms of ramps, lifts, toilets, etc. Helsinki metro is accessible for wheelchair-users, but other forms of public transport may be a bit more problematic, although some city buses "kneel", making it easier to board, and many tram stops are raised. The state railway VR has induction loops and Braille numbering on newer trains.

Assistance is available for wheelchair users by contacting VR customer services (tel: 0800 166 888, www.vr.fi). Wheelchair spaces are limited, so it's best to reserve one ahead of time. When ordering a taxi, specify your needs.

wheelchair **pyörätuoli**
Is there..? **Onko siellä...?**
access for the disabled **esteetön pääsy**
  liikuntaesteisille
a wheelchair ramp **pyörätuoliluiska**
a disabled-accessible toilet **invalidi-WC**

DRIVING

Drive on the right and overtake on the left. Traffic approaching from the right has right of way. Exceptions are on roads marked by a triangle sign; if this is facing you, you must give right of way; similarly, if you are on a very major thoroughfare, it is likely that the feed-in streets will have triangles, giving you the right of way. On roundabouts, the first vehicle to reach the roundabout has right of way.

Speed limits are signposted. Generally the limit in built-up areas is 30kmph (18mph); outside built-up areas, it is usually 80kmph (50mph) unless otherwise indicated; and on motorways 100kmph (62mph) to 120kmph (75mph). In winter, motorway speeds are generally 20kmph (12mph) lower.

Use of headlights is compulsory, even during the daytime (UK cars must sweep their lights right). Wearing of seat belts is also compulsory. A hands-free mobile must be used if you intend to use the phone while driving. Snow tyres are required December to February. Never ever risk driving while drunk in Finland. The limit is very low (0.5 percent blood alcohol) and the fines very steep; imprisonment is also not unheard of.

It is compulsory to carry a warning triangle, to be used in the event of a breakdown. Hazard warning lights should only be used if your vehicle is stranded in a place where it may cause danger to other vehicles.

Is this the way to...? **Meneekö tämä tie... -n/...-lle?**
Can you show me on the map? **Voitteko näyttää minulle kartalta?**
Can I park here? **Voinko pysäköidä tähän?**
My car broke down/won't start. **Autoni meni epäkuntoon/ ei käynnisty.**

E

ELECTRICITY

Finland uses electricity at 220 volts AC (two-pin plug).

EMBASSIES AND CONSULATES

Australia: The nearest Australian embassy is in Stockholm: Klara-bergsviadukten 63, 8th Floor, SE-111 64 Stockholm, tel: (46-8) 613 29 00, http://sweden.embassy.gov.au

Canada: Pohjoisesplanadi 25B, tel: 09 228 530, www.canadainternational.gc.ca

Ireland: Erottajankatu 7A, tel: 09 682 4240, www.irishembassy.fi

New Zealand: The nearest New Zealand embassy is in the Hague: Eisenhowerlaan 77N, 2517 KK The Hague, tel: 31-70 346 93 24

South Africa: Pohjoinen Makasiinikatu 4, tel: 09 6860 3100, www.dirco.gov.za/helsinki

UK: Itäinen Puistotie 17, tel: 09 2286 5100, www.gov.uk/government/world/finland

USA: Itäinen Puistotie 14B, tel: 09 616 250, http://finland.usembassy.gov

EMERGENCIES

The all-purpose emergency number for police, fire, ambulance and rescue services is 112. There's also a 24-hour medical advice hotline, tel: 10 023.

G

GAY AND LESBIAN TRAVELLERS

LGBT lifestyles are readily accepted in Helsinki, though somewhat less so in smaller communities outside the capital. Helsinki has a number of gay nightlife venues. A good resource for gay-friendly bars, clubs, hotels, saunas etc. is the GayMap section of the Swedish lifestyle magazine *QX* (www.qx.se/gaymap). The week-long Helsinki Pride (http://

helsinkipride.fi) is Finland's largest LGBT event. It takes place at the end of June and attracts around 30,000 visitors. Seta (Pasilanraitio 5, 2nd floor, Helsinki; www.seta.fi) is an organisation that campaigns for LGBT equality.

GETTING THERE

Finnair (www.finnair.com) is the national carrier of Finland. In cooperation with British Airways, it operates daily flights between London and Helsinki, between Manchester and Helsinki, and between Edinburgh and Helsinki. Finnair also links with several North American cities including New York. You may be able to find value-for-money package fares and charter flights from New York or London, but they are rare; try the internet sites of the airlines for offers.

Budget airline Norwegian Air (www.norwegian.com) flies year-round between London Gatwick and Helsinki.

GUIDES AND TOURS

Tram Tours. Trams are omnipresent in Helsinki. Trams No. 2 and 3 traces a figure-of-eight course around the centre of Helsinki in roughly one hour, passing many of city's most interesting sights. The tourist office even provides a brochure, "Sightseeing on 2 and 3", for extra self-guided information.

Visitors may find the comforts offered by the **SpåraKOFF** (www.rafla amo.fi/fi/helsinki/sparakoff) more attractive. This is a tram coach converted into a pub, and from its bar you can enjoy refreshments while taking a 40-minute tour of Helsinki's main sights. Running between mid-May and the end of August, the tours start at Railway Square (Tues–Sat at 2pm, 3pm, 5pm, 6pm, 7pm; also in July at 8pm), but you can hop on and off at any of the stops.

Bus Tours. Panorama Sightseeing Bus Tour, which may be arranged as part of the Helsinki Card, tel: 09 2288 1600, www.helsinkicard.com, departs from the Esplanadi Park/Fabianinkatu, lasts 1.75 hours and costs €32. It provides sound effects and commentary in 12 languages, taking in all the most important and interesting sights in Helsinki. It runs at 11am year-round, plus at 1pm in June and July.

Many companies, such as Stromma (www.stromma.fi), offer the **Hop-on Hop-off** open-top bus tours, which depart daily from Senate Square from May to September every 30 to 45 minutes.

Architecture Tours. The tourist office has a free *Jugend Helsinki* brochure and an *Architecture Map* for sale: armed with these two leaflets, you can be your own tour guide to Helsinki's architectural gems. The No. 4 tram also takes you past some interesting buildings, starting from Art-Nouveau-rich Katajanokka and ending in Munkkiniemi.

Architecture buffs should contact *Archtours* (tel: 010 2350 560), a travel agency specialising in tailor-made architecture tours.

Wildlife and Adventure Tours. Natura Viva (tel: 010 292 4030; www.naturaviva.fi) offers guided kayaking trips in the Helsinki archipelago.

If you're here in winter, **Outdoor Helsinki** (tel: 40 53 52 046; www.outdoorhelsinki.fi) can take you skating on the frozen sea, amongst other icy activities.

Both companies offer tours to Nuuksio National Park, just 40km (25 miles) from Helsinki.

H

HEALTH AND MEDICAL CARE

Finland is a very safe country with an excellent health service. Visitors from the EEA are covered for emergency medical treatment on presentation of a European Health Insurance Card (EHIC); take your passport along as well as ID. There is usually a nominal charge for treatment: a visit to a public health centre will cost between €16 and €30, while an overnight hospital stay will cost around €35. Almost any *terveysasema* (public health centre) or *sairaala* (hospital) will treat you.

Non-EEA visitors should arrange health insurance before travelling.

Some pharmacies (*Apteekki*) have late opening hours. In Helsinki, the pharmacy at Mannerheimintie 96, tel. 0300-20 200, has 24-hour service. You can also get round-the-clock medical advice by phoning 09-10023.

Tap water is exceptionally clean and safe to drink.

> I'm sick. **Olen sairas.**
> I need an English-speaking doctor. **Tarvitsen lääkärin,**
>   **joka puhuu englantia.**
> It hurts here. **Tähän sattuu.**

I

INTERNET ACCESS

The city of Helsinki has a free Wi-Fi network with non-passworded hotspots around the city centre (eg. Kluuvi and Kamppi shopping centres, the railway station, Esplanadi). Most hotels also offer free Wi-Fi.

L

LANGUAGE

The official languages of Finland are Finnish and Swedish, spoken by 89 percent and 5 percent of the population respectively.

Most people speak almost perfect English, so you will have no language problems, but mastering a few basic words is always appreciated (see cover flap for Essentials Expressions in Finnish).

M

MEDIA

Newspapers. The Finns are avid devourers of news, and are third in the world for newspaper-readers. The best-selling papers are the Finnish *Helsingin Sanomat* and the tabloid *Ilta-Sanomat*. The largest Swedish-language paper is *Hufvudstadsbladet*.

English-language newspapers usually appear a day or two after UK publication, and can be found in the Central Railway Station, the airport and at least two bookstores (Suomalainen Kirjakauppa at Aleksanterinkatu 23, and Akateeminen Kirjakauppa at Pohjoisesplanadi 39). **Television and Radio.** The Finnish national broadcasting service *Yle* operates four television channels, six national radio stations, and 25 regional radio stations. Short English-language news bulletins can be heard on *Yle Mondo* (97.5 FM in the Helsinki region) at 3.30pm (Mon to Fri) and 3.29pm (Sat and Sun), and also daily at 3.55pm on *YLE Radio 1* (87.9 FM in the Helsinki region). The BBC's World Service and other English-language television channels are usually available in hotels.

MONEY

The Finnish currency is the euro (€), which consists of 100 cents. Bank notes are in denominations of 5, 10, 20, 50, 100, 200 and 500, and there are 1, 2, 5, 10, 20 and 50 cent coins as well as €1 and €2 coins. One- and two-cent coins are not widely used: prices are usually rounded off to the nearest 5.

It's generally easiest to use ATMs or pay with debit or credit cards as you would at home. If you need to exchange money, there are many currency exchange points in Helsinki:

Helsinki-Vantaa Airport: Currency Change Group (tel 09 6940 258) have exchanges in arrival halls 2A (open daily 6am–9pm) and 2B (open daily 7.45am–11pm), and at some gates (15, 26, 32)

Railway Station: Forex (tel: 09 417 1017; Mon–Fri 8am–8pm, Sat 9am–7pm, Sun 9.30am–5pm) and Tavex (Asematunneli; tel: 09 681 49 149; Mon–Fri 10am–6pm)

Stockmann department store also has a currency exchange (8th floor, Aleksanterinkatu 52B; open Mon–Fri 9am–9pm, Sat 9am–7pm, Sun 11am–6pm)

Other places in central Helsinki: Forex (Kauppakeskus Itis Itäkatu 1b, floor -1; tel: 09 417 10385; Mon–Fri 8am–9pm, Sat 9am–7pm, Sun noon–6pm) and Tavex (Fabianinkatu 12; tel: 09 681 49 149; Mon–Fri 9am–6pm, Sat 10am–4pm)

O

OPENING TIMES

Banks are open Monday to Friday 9.15am–4.15pm.

Museums are usually closed on Mondays.

Shops are usually open Monday to Friday 9am–5pm, Saturday 9am–3pm. Some of the bigger department stores and supermarkets stay open until 9pm Monday to Friday and until 6pm on Saturday. Most stores are closed on Sunday, except for those under the Helsinki Railway Station, some in the Forum shopping mall and some on the Esplanadi.

P

POLICE

Helsinki Police Department is located at Pasilanraitio 1, tel: 0295 470 011. Its lost-and-found department is open Mon–Fri 9am–1pm.

The emergency-only number for police, fire, ambulance and rescue services is 112.

POST OFFICES

The main post office is at Elielinaukio 2F (tel: 0200 71000; open Mon–Fri 8am–8pm, Sat–Sun 10am–2pm).

Mail boxes for second-class post are bright orange and widely available. Mail boxes for first-class post are bright blue and less commonly found.

PUBLIC HOLIDAYS

Fixed dates:

1 January *Uudenvuoden päivä* New Year's Day

6 January *Loppiainen* Twelfth Day

1 May *Vapunpäivä* May Day
6 December *Itsenäisyyspäivä* Independence Day
24 December *Jouluaatto* Christmas Eve
25 December *Joulupäivä* Christmas Day
26 December *Tapaninpäiv* Boxing Day
Moveable dates:
Late March/April *Pitkäperjantai* Good Friday
Late March/April *Pääsiäinen* Easter
Late May *Helatorstai* Ascension Day
End May/June *Helluntai* Whitsun
Late June *Juhannus* Midsummer's Day
Early November *Pyhäinpäivä* All Saints' Day

R

RELIGION

The Lutheran Church is the state Church of Finland, with 72 percent of Finns counted as Lutherans. There is a small Greek Orthodox population, and just two Catholic churches in Finland.

In Helsinki, services in English are held at the Rock Church on Lutherinkatu (see page 44); there are both Lutheran and ecumenical services here. There is also one synagogue and one mosque in Helsinki, for those of Jewish or Muslim faith.

As in all places of worship, visitors should dress modestly and behave appropriately.

T

TELEPHONES

Calls to Finland: Dial the international code (00 in Europe, 011 in the US and Canada), then the country code (358), then the town or city area code *without* the initial zero, then the number of the person you are contacting.

Town/city codes: Helsinki 09; Porvoo 019; Tampere 03; Turku 02. To call Tallinn, Estonia, dial the country code 372 before the telephone number.

Calls in Finland: Dial the town/city code and the number of the person you are contacting. For directory enquiries, dial 020202. For overseas call assistance, dial 020208. For information on mobile phones, dial 9800-7000. The few remaining public phone boxes are all card-operated. Hotels usually add surcharges for telephone calls made from your room.

Calls abroad from Finland: Dial 00, then the country code and number, omitting any initial 0 (for example, 00-44 for the UK; 00-1 for US numbers).

Mobile phones: The country is covered by the 900/1800 Mhz GSM network. Most European phones are compatible, although your phone must be unlocked in order to link up with the network. US phones work on a slightly different frequency, so US visitors should check with their phone company first regarding usability. As of 2017, EU roaming charges have been abolished so if you are living in the UK you will not be charged extra for using your data allowance in Finland.

SIM cards: The cheapest way to make calls while in Finland is to buy a prepaid Finnish SIM card and use that in your own mobile phone. For around €10 you can get a SIM card with a Finnish number and €7-worth of talk time. The cards (and refills) can be picked up at any R-Kioski shop. You can also buy prepaid micro SIM cards that can be used in devices such as iPads.

TIME ZONES

Finland is two hours ahead of Greenwich Mean Time (GMT), and seven hours ahead of Eastern Standard Time (USA).

TIPPING

Tipping is not common in Finland. Service charges are included in hotel rates, and in restaurant and taxi prices, so tips are not expected. However, if you have had particularly good service, a tip never goes amiss!

TOILETS

There are 36 automated public toilets throughout Helsinki which cost 50 cents to use; for example, near the Old Market Hall and in Esplanadi.

Men's (*Miehet*) and women's (*Naiset*) toilets are usually distinguished by symbols.

TOURIST INFORMATION

The very helpful **Helsinki City Tourist Information** (Pohjoisesplanadi 19, tel: 09 3101 3300, open mid-May–mid-Sept Mon–Sat 9am–6pm, Sun 9am–4pm; mid-Sept–mid-May Mon–Fri 9am–6pm, Sat–Sun 10am–4pm; www.visithelsinki.fi) will provide you with all the maps, brochures and information that you need to explore the city. There's a smaller branch inside the Central Railway Station (open June–Aug daily 9am–5pm, May and Sept Mon–Fri 9am–4pm, Sat 10am–4pm, Oct–Apr Mon-Fri 9am–3pm, Sat 10am–2pm). In summer, the **Info Container** information booth pops up by the Havis Amanda fountain, next to Market Square, and **Helsinki Helper** tourist guides roam the city-centre streets and cruise-ship harbours looking for lost-looking visitors.

You'll find more general information on Finland as a whole from the Finnish Tourist Board's website **Visit Finland** (www.visitfinland.com).

Helsinki Card. The **Helsinki Card** allows free admission to almost 50 museums and attractions, free travel on public transport in Helsinki (just beep your Helsinki card on the card reader), free travel on the ferry/water-bus to Suomenlinna and Korkeasaari, a free, guided city bus or boat tour, a guide book with maps in five languages, and discounts in some stores and restaurants. It can be purchased online at www.helsinkicard.com, or in person from the tourist office and kiosks and from most hotels. It costs €46 for one day, €56 for two days and €66 for three days, with prices for children (aged 7–16) being €23, €23 and €28 respectively (2017 rates).

Other Tourist Offices:

Fiskars Info is at Fiskarsintie 9, tel: 019 277 7504, www.fiskarsvillage.fi. The community-run information is open year-round Mon–Fri 8am–4pm.

Porvoo City Tourist Office is at Läntinen Aleksanterinkatu 1, tel: 040

489 9801, www.porvoo.fi. The office is open Mon–Fri 9am–6pm, Sat 11am–4pm.

Tampere Tourist Office is at Hämeenkatu 14B (inside the theatre building), tel: 03 5656 6800, www.visittampere.fi. It is open June–Aug Mon–Fri 10am–6pm, Sat–Sun 10am–5pm, Sept–May Mon–Fri 10am–5pm, Sat 10am–3pm.

Turku Tourist Office is at Aurakatu 4, tel: 02 262 7444, www.visitturku.fi. It is open Apr–Sept Mon–Fri 8.30am–6pm, Sat–Sun 9am–4pm; Oct–Mar Mon–Fri 8.30am–6pm, Sat–Sun 10am–3pm.

Tallinn Tourist Information Centre is at Niguliste 2/Kullassepa 4, tel: + 372 645 7777, www.tourism.tallinn.ee. It is open June–Aug Mon–Fri 9am–7pm, Sat–Sun 9am–7pm, Sept, Apr–May Mon–Fri 9am–6pm, Sat–Sun 9am–4pm, Jan–Mar, Oct 9am–5pm, Sat–Sun 9am–3pm.

TRANSPORT

Taxis. All taxis have a yellow *Taksi/Taxi* sign, which, when illuminated, indicates the taxi is vacant. Taxis can be hailed in the street, or there are numerous taxi stands, for instance at Central Railway Station, Senate Square, Esplanade Park and the ferry terminals. To pre-book a taxi, dial 0100 0700) The cost of an advance order is €7.10; this will be added to the fare shown on the meter. The basic day rate (2017 rates) is €5.90, with the increments per kilometre, depending on the number of passengers.

Trams, Buses and Metro. Helsinki's efficient, integrated public transport system is operated by **Helsinki City Transport (HSL),** www.hsl.fi. Individual tram tickets can be bought from the driver for €3.20 or prepaid at ticket machines for €2.50. For the other forms of transport tickets cost €2.90 from a machine. A combined ticket, valid on trams, buses and the metro, costs €9/13.50/18/22.50/27/31.50/36 for one/two/three/four/five/six/seven days. All forms of transport are free for holders of the Helsinki Card (see page 132). Most buses and trams run from around 6am until 1am.

The metro system mainly serves to take commuters to and from the suburbs. Trams are much more convenient for seeing Helsinki's sights.

V

VISA AND ENTRY REQUIREMENTS

Passports and Visas. Citizens belonging to Schengen member states can enter Finland simply with a valid ID card. Most other Western countries, including Ireland, the UK, the US, Canada, Australia and New Zealand, do not need visas to travel to Finland – a passport will suffice, as long as it has been issued within the last 10 years and will remain valid for three months after leaving Finland. Citizens of South Africa do need to obtain a visa before travel from the Embassy of Finland in Pretoria (P.O. Box 443, Pretoria 0001, Republic of South Africa, tel: +27-12-343 0275; www.finland.org.za), and must also have a valid passport, as above.

If you are in any doubt, check the visa requirements on the website of the Ministry for Foreign Affairs in Finland (Ulkoasiainministeriö; http://formin.finland.fi).

Y

YOUTH HOSTELS

Hostelling International Finland (Suomen Retkeilymajajärjestö, SRM; Yrjönkatu 38B 15, 2nd Flr, 00100 Helsinki, tel: 09-565 7150, www.hostellit.fi) oversees three hotels in Helsinki. These are:

Eurohostel (Linnankatu 9, tel: 09-622 0470; www.eurohostel.fi) Next to the Katajanokka ferry terminal. 135 beds. Facilities include launderettes, sauna and café.

Hostel Academica (Hietaniemenkatu 14, tel: 09-1311 4334; www.hostelacademica.fi) Summer-only hostel with 229 small, modern single and twin rooms with their own shower and kitchenette. Residential but central location.

Hostel Suomenlinna (Suomenlinna C 9, tel: 09 684 7471; www.hostelhelsinki.fi) In a stunning location within the Suomenlinna Fortress. Sleeps 40 in dorms and three private rooms.

RECOMMENDED HOTELS

Hotels in Helsinki are a homogenous bunch of comfortable, unremarkable chain hotels. Most of them lie within a broad stripe sweeping from Senate Square west to the end of Bulevardi. A further handful are dotted here and there off Mannerheimintie, and the quiet residential Katajanokka district holds another clutch. Another couple lie behind the cathedral and near Hakaniemi Market. Most hotels are within easy walking distance, or at the very most a 15-minute bus- or tram-ride, from the city centre.

Helsinki is so small that there is no special benefit to staying in one area or another, apart from personal preference. Would you like your surroundings to be neoclassical or Jugendstil? Would you prefer a sea view or one of Töölönlahti Bay?

Hotels are listed below first by area, in the order covered in the Where to Go chapter, and then alphabetically.

Approximate prices for a double room in high season:

€€€€	Over €250
€€€	€150–250
€€	€75–150
€	Under €75

RAUTATIENTORI

Holiday Inn Helsinki City Centre €€€€ *Elielinaukio 5, tel: 020 048 103;* www.ihg.com. Courteous staff and a clean, modern environment make this large hotel a very good central choice. The Finnair airport bus terminates right outside. Some rooms overlook the bus station, but excellent sound-proofing means you don't hear a thing. Facilities include air-conditioning, a restaurant, lobby bar and two saunas.

Radisson Blu Plaza Hotel €€€ *Mikonkatu 23, tel: 020 1234 703;* www. radissonblu.com. Next to Central Railway Station and the Finnish National Theatre, this hotel occupies a building dating from 1917 that has been renovated to include up-to-date facilities. The 302 air-conditioned rooms include six suites and six rooms for people with disabilities. Cheaper room prices are available that do not include breakfast.

Seurahuone €€€ *Kaivokatu 12, tel: 020 048 106;* www.hotelliseurahuone. fi. This is one of Helsinki's most emblematic hotels. Opened in 1833, it was moved to its present position opposite the Central Railway Station in 1914, and well-preserved Jugendstil features give it a singular atmosphere. There are 114 rooms and four suites, mostly non-smoking. It also has a bistro, bar and saunas.

MARKET SQUARE AND ESPLANADI

Fabian €€€-€€€€ *Fabianinkatu 7, tel: 09 6128 2000;* www.hotelfabian.fi. The Fabian's slogan is "We don't mind if you stay longer" – and you certainly won't mind either. The 58-room boutique hotel is one of Helsinki's best and brightest, with chic rooms full of clever design details. Its Lux rooms, some with private entrances, are designed for longer stays and come with kitchenettes. Conveniently located, two blocks away from the Old Market Hall.

GLO Hotel €€€ *Kluuvikatu 4, tel: 010 344 4400;* www.glohotels.fi. This unique boutique hotel right off Alexanterinkatu features sizeable modern rooms, with large beds, exposed wood and shimmering black marble. Its services are what the hotel is really known for – there's even a menu of unusual items that you can order to your room: gym equipment, painting equipment, spa treatments or even a guitar.

Haven €€€€ *Unioninkatu 17, tel: 09-681 930,* www.hotelhaven.fi. Helsinki's design hotel changed the face of luxury accommodation in the city when it opened in 2009. It's a refined option right at the harbourside, with a leather-outfitted lobby is an honesty bar, fireplace and a library of leather-bound books. Rooms look onto the Uspenski Cathedral, and offer Egyptian cotton linens, Bang & Olufsen TVs and Elemis bath products. Free bicycles are available for guests to use.

Kämp Hotel €€€€ *Pohjoisesplanadi 29, tel: 09 576 111;* www.hotelkamp.com. Opened in 1887, this central neoclassical five-star boasts 189 Belle Epoque rooms and suites with marble bathrooms, polished stonework and lavish furnishings that all evoke a very decadent glamour. There is a gourmet restaurant and a comfortable, relaxing bar.

KATAJANOKKA

Eurohostel € *Linnankatu 9, tel: 09-622 0470;* www.eurohostel.fi. Next to the Katajanokka ferry terminal, this no-frills hostel has 135 rooms with shared facilities, as well as launderettes, sauna and café. Convenient for those travelling by ship, and just 10 minutes' walk from the centre.

Katajanokka €€€ *Merikasarminkatu 1A, tel: 09 686 45132;* www.hotelkatajanokka.fi. Best Western Premier hotel is a fabulous choice with a unique history, being the only Helsinki hotel set in a former prison. The layout is preserved and the well-soundproofed rooms are done up in designer furnishings and linens. Tram No. 4 runs here from the city centre, a journey of about 10 minutes – get off at the Vyökatu stop.

Scandic Grand Marina €€€€ *Katajanokanlaituri 7, tel: 09 16 661;* www.scandichotels.com. Designed in 1911 by noted Finnish architect Lars Sonck, this Katajanokka hotel offers 470 exquisitely decorated and well-equipped rooms, plus extensive conference facilities, numerous restaurants and a heated garage. One of Helsinki's newest attractions, the FINNAIR SkyWheel, revolves slowly outside.

KAMPPI

Finn €€ *Kalevankatu 3 B, tel: 09 684 4360;* www.hotellifinn.fi. This is one of the city's smallest hotels, with just 35 rooms. Its central location and low prices make it a good budget choice. Rooms are small, but clean and functional. Breakfast (extra cost) is served at a restaurant next door.

Helka Hotel €€ *Pohjoinen Rautatiekatu 23, tel: 09 613 580;* www.helka.fi. A medium-sized independent hotel, within easy walking distance of the

Central Railway Station. Helka has 150 rooms, all of which are decorated in a spare, modern Scandinavian style, with furniture designed by Alvar Aalto, and giant photos of Finnish nature stuck to the ceiling! The buffet breakfast here is a stand-out affair.

Hostel Academica € *Hietaniemenkatu 14, tel: 09-1311 4334;* www.hostel academica.fi. This HI-affiliated summer-only hostel has 326 small, modern single and twin rooms with their own shower, plus a kitchenette and fridge. Family rooms and extra beds are also available. Breakfast costs an extra €9.5. The hostel is on a peaceful residential street.

Omena Hotelli €€ *Eerikinkatu 24 and Lönnrotinkatu 13, tel: 0600 555 222 (€9 booking fee when you make a phone reservation);* www.omena.com. These two central Omena hotels are good for thrifty groups or families. Prices are per room, each one furnished with a double bed and two fold-out singles, plus kitchenettes containing a microwave, kettle, coffee machine and fridge. Decor is simple but pleasant, with deep, dark woods. The chain saves on costs by avoiding reception staff: entry is by code, which you are given upon booking. Eerikinkatu is behind the Forum shopping centre, while Lönnrotinkatu is a few streets away by the Old Church.

Radisson Blu Royal €€€€ *Runeberginkatu 2, tel: 20 123 4701;* www.radis sonblu.com. Recently renovated rooms and sunny open dining and bar areas. A favourite with business travellers, and its location next to the Kamppi complex makes it handy for shopping, restaurants and nightclubs.

Scandic Hotel Simonkenttä €€€ *Simonkatu 9, tel: 09 68 380;* www. scandichotels.com. This is a large, elegant hotel with modern architecture and ecological design. It's right by the bus station so consider getting a room on the 4th floor or above to lessen street noise – and, of course, to enjoy fine views over the city centre. The restaurant serves international and Scandinavian cuisine, and there's a roof-top pavilion, three saunas and a gymnasium.

Sokos Hotel Torni €€€ *Yrjönkatu 26, tel: 020 1234 604;* www.sokoshotels. fi. Helsinki's tallest building, with 13 floors, opened in 1931 and has rooms in both its Art Deco and Jugendstil buildings – try for those over-looking the courtyard. Its restaurants and bars include the Ateljé (see page 112), with its panoramic views, the American Bar, an international cocktail bar, and O'Malley's, the city's oldest Irish bar. There are also four saunas.

MANNERHEIMINTIE

Helsinki Apartment €€ *Töölöntorinkatu 7, tel: 050 367 6916;* www.helsinkiapartment.fi. These comfortable and stylish apartments offer an excellent alternative to anonymous Helsinki hotel rooms. The bright rooms contain classic Scandinavian furniture, and have kitchens/kitchenettes and access to laundry facilities. Most of the 15 apartments, located around Kamppi and Töölöntori, are one- and two-bedroomed, but larger options are available. Possibly the best bargain in the city.

Scandic Park €€€–€€€€ *Mannerheimintie 46, tel: 09 47 371;* www.scandichotels.com. Directly across from Hesperia Park, this is a five-star affair. Economy and standard rooms keep things simple, with wooden floors and soothing colour schemes; superior rooms overlook the bay and are tremendously peaceful. The hotel has a swimming pool, and a swishy rooftop hot tub.

THE "DESIGN DISTRICT"

Anna €€ *Annankatu 1, tel: 09-616 621;* www.hotelanna.com. This quiet, decently-priced hotel, with 64 comfortable rooms, is set in a shopping quarter in the city centre. A good place for people travelling alone – almost half the rooms are singles.

Holiday Inn Hotel Indigo *Bulevardi 26, tel: 020 048 105;* www.ihg.com. Award-winning Indigo has 120 boutique rooms, exuding chic Scandistyle. Some of its public areas have had input from up-and-coming Helsinki fashion designer Satu Maaranen. Facilities include a Body, Mind & Soul studio, a fitness centre and a yoga trapeze. The hotel also has an environmental focus: charging points for electric cars and a highly energy efficient LEED® environmental classification rating.

Hostel Diana Park Erottajanpuisto € *Uudenmaankatu 9, tel: 09 642 169;* www.erottajanpuisto.com. This dinky HI hostel has a warm, welcoming atmosphere and cosy rooms, whether you choose an eight-bed dormitory or a private double. It's deservedly popular, so book ahead. A 10-minute walk from the railway station; trams 3B and 6 run close by.

Klaus K €€€ *Bulevardi 2-4, tel: 020 770 4700;* www.klauskhotel.com. Top-of-the-class Klaus K is a chic, family-run boutique hotel. Its small but gorgeous rooms are decorated with a Kalevala-inspired theme, and come with every amenity. They're a breath of fresh air amongst Helsinki's often rather bland hotel options. The Sky Lofts have access to a rooftop terrace.

Radisson Blu Seaside Hotel €€€ *Ruoholahdenranta 3, tel: 020 1234 707;* www.radissonblu.com. Near the bottom of Bulevardi and Hietalahti Market, the Radisson has pleasing views over the western harbour and offers 349 modern, comfortable rooms. It's about 2.5km (1.5 miles) from the railway station – trams Nos. 6 and 9 stop outside. A good option if you're catching an early ferry to Tallinn.

Rivoli Jardin €€€€ *Kasarmikatu 40, tel: 09 681 500;* www.rivoli.fi. In a townhouse right in the heart of the business and shopping area, this 55-room hotel is quiet, clean and has a faintly old-fashioned feel. Rooms are tastefully furnished with all amenities; a buffet breakfast is included, although internet costs extra.

KALLIO

Hilton Helsinki Strand €€€€ *John Stenbergin ranta 4, tel: 09 39 351;* www.helsinki-strand.hilton.com. Just across the Pitkäsilta Bridge from the Botanic Gardens, the Hilton features an impressive atrium with glass lifts. Service is exemplary, and there is an indoor swimming pool.

Scandic Paasi €€€–€€€€. *Paasivuorenkatu 5 B, tel: 09 2311 700,* www.scandichotels.fi. Close to Hakaniemi Market, and overlooking Eläintarhanlahti Bay, this hotel is packed with personality. Room decor is inspired by the area's colourful history, and there is a library and bicycle-borrowing scheme for guests.

SUOMENLINNA

Hostel Suomenlinna € *Suomenlinna C 9, tel: 09 684 7471;* www.hostel helsinki.fi. The hostel itself is pleasant but basic; but as it's the only place to stay within Suomenlinna Fortress, it's worth staying here for the novelty factor alone – you get to enjoy this Unesco World Heritage site when all the other tourists have caught the boat back to the mainland. Sleeps 38 in dorms and eight private rooms.

FURTHER AFIELD

Hilton Helsinki Kalastajatorppa €€€€ *Kalastajatorpantie 1, tel: 09 45 811;* www.hilton.com. This well-known business hotel has 238 comfortable rooms, each with a view of the sea or the verdant park around it. The hotel has its own private beach and six tennis courts. It's out of the city centre, close to Akseli Gallén-Kallela's house Tarvaspää, but is linked to central Helsinki by a 20-minute ride on trams Nos. 4 or 4T.

DICTIONARY

ENGLISH – FINNISH

adj adjective **adv** adverb **BE** British English **n** noun **prep** preposition **v** verb

A

a (with common nouns) (articles do not exist in Finnish)
a (with neuter nouns) (articles do not exist in Finnish)
able kyvykäs
about noin
above yllä, yli, yläpuolella
accept v **(approval)** hyväksyä
access n pääsy
accessory asuste
accident onnettomuus
account tili
ache särky
acupuncture akupunktio
adapter sovitin
address n osoite
admission (sisään)pääsy
admitted päästää sisään
after jälkeen
afternoon iltapäivä
aftershave lotion partavesi
again uudelleen
against vastaan
age ikä
air conditioning ilmastointi
air mattress ilmapatja
airmail lentoposti
airplane lentokone
airport lentokenttä, lentoasema

aisle seat käytäväpaikka
alarm clock herätyskello
alcohol alkoholi
alcoholic adj alkoholi-
allergic allerginen
allergic reaction allerginen reaktio
alphabet aakkoset
also myös
alter v korjata
altitude sickness vuoristotauti
amazing hämmästyttävä
amber meripihka
ambulance ambulanssi
American amerikkalainen
amethyst ametisti
amount v **(money)** summa
amusement park huvipuisto
analgesic kipua lievittävä
and ja
anesthetic puudutusaine
animal eläin
ankle nilkka
answer vastaus
antibiotic antibiootti
antidepressant mielialalääke
antique antiikki
antiques store antiikkiliike
antiseptic cream antiseptinen voide
any yhtään

anyone kukaan
anything mitään
anywhere jossain, missään
apartment asunto
aperitif aperitiivi
appendix umpilisäke (anatomy)
appliance kodinkone
appointment sovittu tapaaminen, aika
arcade pelihalli
architect arkkitehti
arm käsivarsi
aromatherapy aromaterapia
around (approximately); (around the corner) suunnilleen; ympäri
arrival saapuvat
arrive olla perillä, saapua, tulla
art taide
art gallery taidegalleria
aspirin aspiriini
assistance apu
assorted sekalainen
asthma astma
astringent kasvovesi
at kohdalla
ATM pankkiautomaatti
attack n hyökkäys
attend osallistua
attractive viehättävä
audio guide ääniopas

Australia Australia
average keskinkertainen
away pois
awful kaamea

B

baby vauva
baby bottle tuttipullo
baby food vauvanruoka
baby wipes kosteuspyyhkeet
babysitter back selkä
backache selkäsärky
backpack reppu
bad huono, kehno
bag (purse/(handbag)); (shopping) laukku; kassi
baggage (BE) matkatavara
baggage check (työntö) kärry
baggage claim matkatavaran nouto
bakery leipomo
balance (finance) saldo
balcony parveke
ballet ballet baletti
bandage n side
bank (finance) pankki
bank note seteli
bar baari
barber parturi
basket kori
basketball game koripallo-ottelu

bath kylpy
bathing suit uimapuku
bathrobe kylpytakki
bathroom kylpyhuone
battery akku, paristo
battleground taistelukenttä
be olla
beach ball rantapallo
beard parta
beautiful kaunis
beauty salon kauneu-
shoitola
bed vuode
before (time) ennen
begin alkaa
behind takana, taakse
beige beige
bell (electric) soittokello
below alla, alle
belt vyö
berth makuupaikka,
vuodepaikka
better parempi
between välissä, välillä
bicycle (polku)pyörä
big suuri, iso
bike route pyöräilyreitti
bikini bikini
**bill (restaurant); (bank
note)** lasku; seteli
binoculars kiikari
bird lintu
birth syntymä
birthday syntymäpäivä
black musta
bladder virtsarakko
blade terä
blanket peitto
bleach valkaisuaine
bleed vuotaa verta
blind (window) kaihdin
blister rakko
blocked tukossa
blood veri

blood pressure
verenpaine
blouse pusero
blow dry föönaus
blue sininen
boat vene, lautta, alus
boat trip venematka
body ruumis
bone luu
book kirja
booklet (of tickets)
lippuvihko
bookstore kirjakauppa
boot saapas
boring ikävystyttävä
born syntynyt
botanical garden kasvitieteellinen puutarha
botany kasvitiede
bother häiritä
bottle pullo
bottle opener pul-
lonavaaja
bottom alaosa
bowel suoli
bowl kulho
box laatikko
boxing match nyrk-
keilyottelu
boy poika
boyfriend poikaystävä
bra rintaliivit
bracelet rannekoru
brake n jarru
break (out of order)
mennä rikki
breakdown (car)
konerikko
breakfast aamiainen
breast rinta
breathe hengittää
bridge silta
bring tuoda
bring down tuoda alas
British (person) britti

broken rikki, murtunut
brooch rintakoru
broom luuta
brown ruskea
bruise mustelma
brush n harja
bucket ämpäri
bug ötökkä
build rakentaa
building rakennus
burn palohaava
bus linja-auto
bus station linja-
autoasema
bus stop linja-
autopysäkki
business card
käyntikortti
**business center (at
hotel)** liiketoi-
mintakeskus
business class
business-luokka
business district
liikekeskus
business trip liikematka
busy kiireinen
but mutta
butane gas butaani,
nestekaasu
butcher lihakauppa
button nappi
buy ostaa

C

cabin (ship) hytti
cafe kahvila
calculator laskin
calendar kalenteri
call n (phone); v; (summon) puhelu; kutsua
calm rauhallinen
camera kamera
camera case kamera-
laukku

camera shop valoku-
vausliike
camp bed leirintävuode
camp v leiriytyä
camping leirintä
camping equipment
leirintävarusteet
campsite leirintäpaikka
can opener tölkinavaaja
can v (be able to);
(container) n pystyä;
tölkki
Canada Kanada
Canadian kanadalainen
cancel peruuttaa
candle kynttilä
candy store
makeiskauppa
cap lakki
car auto
car hire [BE] auton-
vuokraus
car mechanic (auton)
korjaaja
car park [BE] pysäköintialue
car rental auton-
vuokraus
car seat turvaistuin
carafe karahvi
card kortti
card game korttipeli
cardigan neuletakki
carry kantaa
cart (työntö)kärry
carton (of cigarettes)
kartonki
case (camera) (kamera)
laukku
cash v; n lunastaa;
käteinen
cashier kassa
casino kasino
castle slot; linna
caution varoitus

cave luola
CD CD-levy
cell phone matkapuhelin
cemetery hautausmaa
center of town kaupungin keskusta
centimeter senttimetri
ceramics keramiikka
certain varma
certificate todistus
chair tuoli
change n (money); v (money); (clothes, diaper) vaihtoraha; vaihtaa (rahaa); vaihtaa (vaatteet, vaippa)
charcoal grillihiili
charge n; v maksu; veloittaa
cheap halpa
check (restaurant) n; **(banking)** v (someone, something) lasku; šekki; tarkistaa
check-in desk (airport) lähtöselvitys
checking account käyttötili
check out v huoneen luovutus
check-up (medical) lääkärintarkastus
cheers kippis
chef keittiömestari
chemical toilet kemiallinen WC
chemist [BE] apteekki
cheque [BE] šekki
chess šakki
chess set šakkipeli
chest rintakehä
chest pain rintakipu
child barn lapsi
child's seat lastenistuin
children's clothing

lastenvaatteet
children's portion lastenannos
choice valinta
church kirkko
cigar sikari
cigarette savuke
cinema [BE] elokuvateatteri
classical klassinen
clean adj; v puhdas; puhdistaa
cleansing cream puhdistusvoide
clear v selvittää
cliff jyrkänne
clip liitin
clock kello
close v sulkea
closed suljettu
cloth kangas
clothing vaatteet
clothing store vaatekauppa
cloud pilvi
coat n (clothing) takki
coin kolikko
cold (illness) adj vilustuminen; kylmä
collar kaulus
colleague työtoveri
color väri
comb kampa
come tulla
comedy komedia
commission (fee) välityspalkkio
common (frequent) yleinen
compartment (train) vaununosasto
compass kompassi
complaint valitus
computer (PC) tietokone
concert konsertti

concert hall konserttisali
condom kondomi
conference room kokoushuone
confirm vahvistaa
confirmation vahvistus
congratulations onnittelut
connect v yhdistää
connection (transportation, internet) yhteys
constipation ummetus
consulate konsulaatti
contact lens piilolinssi
contagious tarttuva
contain sisältää
contraceptive ehkäisyväline
contract sopimus
control tarkastus
convention hall kokoussali
cooking facilities ruoanlaittomahdollisuus
copper kupari
corkscrew korkkiruuvi
corner kulma
cost n; v maksu; maksaa
cot lapsen sänky
cotton puuvilla
cough n yskä
counter tiski
country maa
countryside maaseutu
court house oikeustalo
cover charge palvelumaksu
cramps kuukautiskivut
crayon värikynä
cream (toiletry) voide
credit saldo **(prepaid telephone)**, luotto **(payment)**
credit card luottokortti
crib vauvan sänky

crockery [BE] astiat
cross-country skiing murtomaahiihto
crossing (maritime) ylitys
crossroads tienhaara
crown (Danish currency) kruunu
crystal kristalli
cufflink kalvosinnappi
cuisine keittiö
cup kuppi
currency valuutta
currency exchange office valuutanvaihto(toimisto)
current (ocean) merivirta
curtain verho
customs tulli
customs declaration form tullauslomake
cut n (wound); v (with scissors) haava; leikata
cut glass hiottu lasi
cycling race pyöräilykisa

D

dairy meijeri
damaged vaurioitunut
dance club yökerho
dance n; v tanssi; tanssia
danger vaara
dangerous vaarallinen
Danish (person) adj tanskalainen
dark pimeä, tumma
date (appointment); (day) treffit; päivämäärä
day päivä
decision päätös
deck (ship) kansi
deck chair kansituoli

declare (customs) tullata

deep syvä

degree (temperature) aste

delay viivytys

delicatessen herkkumyymälä

delicious herkullinen

deliver toimittaa

delivery toimitus

denim farkkukangas

Denmark Tanska

dentist hammaslääkäri

denture hammasproteesi

deodorant deodorantti

depart lähteä

department (shop) osasto

department store tavaratalo

departure lähtö

departure gate lähtöportti

deposit n (bank); (down payment) pano; ennakkomaksu

dessert jälkiruoka

detergent pesuaine

detour (traffic) kiertotie

diabetic diabeetikko

diamond timantti

diaper vaippa

diarrhea ripuli

dictionary sanakirja

diesel dieselöljy

diet ruokavalio

difficult vaikea

digital digitaalinen

dining car ravintolavaunu

dining room ruokasali

dinner päivällinen

direct adj; v (someone) suora; opastaa

direction suunta

directory (phone) puhelinluettelo

dirty likainen

disabled vammainen

disc (parking) pysäköintikiekko

disconnect v (computer) irrottaa

discount alennus

disease tauti

dish (food item) ruokalaji

dishes (plates) astiat

dishwasher astianpesukone

dishwashing detergent astianpesuaine

disinfectant desinfiointiaine

display case vitriini

district (of town) alue

disturb häiritä

divorced eronnut

dizzy huimaantunut

doctor lääkäri

doctor's office lääkärin vastaanotto

dog koira

doll nukke

dollar (U.S.) dollari

domestic (airport terminal) kotimaa

domestic flight kotimaanlento

double bed parivuode

double room kahden hengen huone

down alhaalla, alas

downtown area keskusta-alue

dozen tusina

dress n leninki, mekko

drink n; (cocktail); v juoma; juoda

drinking water juomavesi

drip tippua

drive ajaa

driver's license ajokortti

drop (liquid) tippa

drugstore apteekki

dry kuiva

dry cleaner kuivapesula

dummy [BE] (baby's) tutti

during aikana

duty (customs) tulli

duty-free goods verovapaat tavarat

duty-free shop verovapaa myymälä

dye värjätä

E

each joka

ear korva

ear drops korvatipat

earache korvasärky

early aikainen, aikaisin

earring korvakoru

east itä

easy helppo

eat syödä

economy class economy-luokka

elastic elastinen

electric sähköinen

electrical outlet sähköpistorasia

electricity sähkö

electronic elektroninen

elevator hissi

e-mail sähköposti

e-mail address sähköpostiosoite

embassy suurlähetystö

embroidery kirjailu

emerald smaragdi

emergency hätä

emergency exit hätäuloskäynti

empty tyhjä

enamel emali

end loppu

engaged (phone) varattu

England Englanti

English (language); (person) englannin kieli; englantilainen

enjoyable viihtyisä

enlarge suurentaa

enough tarpeeksi

enter v mennä sisään

entrance sisäänkäynti

entrance fee pääsymaksu

entry (access) sisäänpääsy

envelope kirjekuori

equipment varusteet

eraser pyyhekumi

escalator rullaportaat

estimate n; v (quotation) arvio; arvioida

e-ticket e-lippu

e-ticket check-in lähtöselvitys e-lipulla

Europe Eurooppa

European Union Euroopan unioni

evening ilta

every joka

everything kaikki

exchange rate vaihtokurssi

exchange v (money) vaihtaa (rahaa)

excursion retki

excuse v suoda anteeksi

exhibition näyttely

exit n; v (computer) uloskäynti; poistua

expect odottaa

expense kulu

expensive kallis

express pika

expression ilmaisu
extension (phone) alanumero
extra lisä
eye silmä
eye drops silmätipat
eye shadow luomiväri
eyesight näkö

F

fabric (cloth) kangas
face kasvot
facial kasvohoito
factory tehdas
fair messut (expo), vaalea (light), reilu (just)
fall v kaatua
family perhe
fan tuuletin
far kaukana
fare (ticket) maksu
farm maatila
far-sighted kaukonäköinen
fast adj nopea
fast-food place pikaruokapaikka
faucet vesihana
fax faksi
fax number faksinumero
fee (commission) välityspalkkio
feed v syöttää
feel (physical state) olo
ferry lautta
fever kuume
few harva
field pelto, kenttä
file (for nails) viila
fill in (form) täyttää
filling (tooth) paikka
film [BE] filmi
filter suodatin
find v löytää
fine (OK) hyvin, hyvä

fine arts taiteet
finger sormi
fire tuli(palo)
fire door palo-ovi
fire escape palopakotie
fire exit palouloskäynti
first ensimmäinen
first-aid kit ensiapupakkaus
first class ensimmäinen luokka
first course ensimmäinen ruokalaji
fishing kalastus
fitting room sovituskoppi
fix v korjata, paikata
flashlight taskulamppu
flat [BE] (apartment) asunto
flatware aterimet
flea market kirpputori
flight lento
floor lattia (of a room), kerros (of a building)
florist kukkakauppias
flower kukka
flu flunssa
fluid neste
fog sumu
follow seurata
food ruoka
food poisoning ruokamyrkytys
foot jalka
football [BE] jalkapallo
for suuntaan, sijaan
forbidden kielletty
forecast ennuste
foreign ulkomainen
forest metsä
forget unohtaa
fork haarukka
form (document) kaavake

fountain lähde
frame (glasses) kehykset
free ilmainen (of charge), vapaa (not restricted)
freezer pakastin
fresh tuore (of food), raikas (of air and water)
friend ystävä
from suunnasta
frost pakkanen
frying pan paistinpannu
full täysi
full-time kokoaikainen
furniture huonekalut

G

gallery galleria
game peli
garage autotalli, korjaamo
garbage roska
garden puutarha
gas kaasu
gasoline bensiini
gauze sideharso
gem jalokivi
general yleinen
general delivery poste restante
general practitioner [BE] yleislääkäri
genuine aito
get (find) saada
get off jäädä pois
get up nousta ylös
gift lahja
gift shop lahjatavarakauppa
girl tyttö
girlfriend tyttöystävä
give antaa
gland rauhanen

glass (drinking) lasi
glasses (optical) silmälasit
glove hansikas
glue liima
go away mennä pois
go back mennä takaisin
go out mennä ulos (literally), sammua (of a flame)
gold kulta
golf club golfmaila
golf course golfkenttä
golf tournament golfturnaus
good hyvä
good afternoon hyvää iltapäivää
good evening hyvää iltaa
good morning hyvää huomenta
good night hyvää yötä
goodbye hyvästi
gram gramma
grandchild lastenlapsi
gray harmaa
great (excellent) hieno
Great Britain Iso-Britannia
green vihreä
greengrocer's [BE] vihannesmyymälä
greeting tervehdys
ground-floor room [BE] ensimmäisen kerroksen huone
groundsheet telttapatja
group ryhmä
guesthouse matkustajakoti
guide dog opaskoira
guide n opas
guidebook opaskirja
gym kuntosali
gynecologist gynekologi

H

hair hiukset
hair dryer hiustenkuivain
hairbrush hiusharja
haircut tukanleikkuu
hairdresser kampaaja
hairspray hiuskiinne
hall (room) sali
hammer vasara
hammock riippumatto
hand käsi
hand cream käsivoide
hand washable käsinpestävä
handbag [BE] käsilaukku
handicrafts käsityö(tuotteet)
handkerchief nenäliina
handmade käsin tehty
hanger (vaate)ripustin
happy iloinen, onnellinen
harbor satama
hard kova
hardware store rautakauppa
hare jänis
hat hattu
have (must); (possess) täytyä; omistaa
hay fever heinänuha
head pää
headache päänsärky
headlight ajovalo
headphones kuulokkeet
health food store luontaistuotemyymälä
health insurance sairausvakuutus
hearing-impaired kuulovammainen
heart sydän
heart attack sydänkohtaus
heat v lämmittää
heating lämmitys

heavy raskas, painava
hello hei
helmet kypärä
help; (oneself) auttaa; ottaa
here täällä
hi hei
high adj korkea
high tide korkea vuorovesi
highchair syöttötuoli
highway moottoritie
hill mäki
hire [BE] v vuokrata
history historia
hole reikä
holiday; [BE] pyhäpäivä; loma
home koti
horseback riding ratsastus
hospital sairaala
hot (temperature) kuuma
hotel hotelli
hotel directory hotelliopas
hotel reservation hotellin varaus
hour (time) tunti
house talo
how kuinka
how far kuinka kaukana
how long kuinka kauan
how many kuinka monta
how much kuinka paljon
hug v halata
hungry nälkäinen
hunting metsästys
hurry kiirehtiä
hurt loukata
husband aviomies

I

I minä
ice jää

icy (weather) jäinen
identification (card) henkilöllisyystodistus
if jos
ill [BE] sairas
illness sairaus
important tärkeä
imported maahantuotu
impressive vaikuttava
in sisässä, sisällä
include sisältää
indoor sisä-
inexpensive huokea
infected tulehtunut
infection tulehdus
inflammation tulehdus
information neuvonta
information desk neuvontapiste
injection ruiske
injure loukata
injury vamma
inn majatalo
innocent viaton
inquiry tiedustelu
insect bite hyönteisen pisto
insect repellent hyönteismyrkky
insect spray hyönteissuihke
inside sisässä, sisälle
instant messenger instant messenger pikaviestin
insurance vakuutus
insurance claim vakuutushakemus
interest (finance) korko
interested kiinnostunut
interesting mielenkiintoinen
international; (airport terminal) ulkomaat

international flight kansainvälinen lento
internet internet
internet cafe internet-kahvila
interpreter tulkki
intersection risteys
introduce esitellä
introduction (social) esittely
investment sijoitus
invitation kutsu
invite v kutsua
invoice lasku
iodine jodi
Ireland Irlanti
Irish (person); adj irlantilainen
iron n (clothing); v silitysrauta; silittää
itemized bill eritelty lasku

J

jacket jakku
jar (container) purkki
jaw leuka
jazz jazz
jeans farkut
jet ski vesiskootteri
jeweler kultasepänliike
join v liittää
joint (anatomy) nivel
journey matka
just (only) vain

K

keep pitää
kerosene kerosiini
key avain
key card avainkortti
kiddie pool lastenallas
kidney munuainen
kilogram kilogramma
kilometer kilometri

kind adj; n ystävällinen; laatu
kiss v suudella
knee polvi
knife veitsi
knitwear neule
knock koputtaa
know tietää

L

label etiketti
lace pitsi
lactose intolerant laktoosi-intolerantikko
lake järvi
lamp lamppu
landscape maisema
language kieli
lantern lyhty
large suuri
last viimeinen
late (time); (delay) myöhään; myöhässä
laugh nauraa
launderette [BE] itsepalvelupesula
laundromat itsepalve-lupesula
laundry pesula
laundry facilities vaatteidenpesumah-dollisuus
laundry service pesulapalvelu
lawyer lakimies
laxative ulostuslääke
leather nahka
leave v; (behind) lähteä; jättää
left vasen
left-luggage office [BE] matkatavaran säilytys
leg jalka
lens (camera);

(glasses) linssi
less vähemmän
lesson oppitunti
letter kirje (message); kirjain (of the alphabet)
library kirjasto
license (driving) ajokortti
life boat pelastusvene
life guard (beach) hengenpelastaja
life jacket pelastusliivi
life preserver pelastus-rengas
lift [BE] elevator hissi
light (color); (weight) vaalea; kevyt
light bulb hehkulamppu
lighter sytytin (tool used to produce a flame); vaaleampi (color); kevyempi (weight)
lightning salama
like; (please) pitää; miellyttää
linen pellava
lip huuli
lipstick huulipuna
liquor store viinakauppa; Alko (the chain in Finland)
listen kuunnella
liter litra
little (amount) vähän
live v elää (to be alive), asua (to stay)
loafers louferit
local paikallinen
log off kirjautua ulos
log on kirjautua sisään
login kirjautua sisään
long pitkä
long-sighted [BE] kaukonäköinen

look v katsoa
lose menettää (forgo), kadottaa (misplace)
loss menetys
lost menetetty (forgone), kadotettu (misplaced)
lost and found löytötä-varatoimisto
lost property office [BE] löytötavaratoimisto
lotion kosteusemulsio
loud (voice) kova
love v rakastaa
lovely ihana
low matala
low tide matala vuorovesi
luck onni
luggage matkatavarat
luggage cart (työntö) kärry
luggage locker säilytyslokero
lunch lounas
lung keuhko

M

magazine aikakauslehti
magnificent suuren-moinen
maid siivooja
mail n; v posti; postittaa
mailbox postilaatikko
make-up n meikki
mall ostoskeskus
mallet nuija
man mies
manager johtaja
manicure manikyyri
many monta
map kartta
market n (kauppa)tori
married naimisissa
mass (religious service) messu

massage hieronta
match n (sport) ottelu
material materiaali
matinée matinea
mattress patja
may v saattaa
meadow niitty
meal ateria
mean v tarkoittaa
measure mitata
measuring cup mit-takuppi
measuring spoon mittalusikka
mechanic mekaaninen (adjective), korjaaja (person)
medicine (drug) lääke
meet tavata
memorial muistomerkki
memory card muistikortti
mend korjata
menu; ruokalista
message viesti
meter metri
middle keski-
midnight keskiyö
mileage kilometrimäärä
minute minuutti
mirror peili
miscellaneous sekalaiset
Miss neiti
miss v (lacking) puuttua
mistake virhe
mobile phone [BE] matkapuhelin
moisturizing cream kosteusvoide
moment hetki
money raha
money order mak-sumääräys
month kuukausi

monument muistomerkki
moon *n* kuu
mop *n* moppi
moped mopo
more lisää
morning aamu
mosque moskeija
mosquito net hyttysverkko
motel motelli
motorboat moottorivene
motorcycle moottoripyörä
motorway [BE] moottoritie
moustache viikset
mouth suu
mouthwash suuvesi
move *v* liikkua (self), liikuttaa (other)
movie elokuva
Mr. herra
Mrs. rouva
much paljon
mug *n* muki
mugging ryöstö
muscle lihas
museum museo
music musiikki
musical musikaali
must (have to) täytyä

N

nail (body) kynsi
nail clippers kynsileikkuri
nail file kynsiviila
nail salon kynsihoitola
name nimi
napkin lautasliina
nappy [BE] vaippa
narrow kapea
nationality kansallisuus
natural luonnollinen
nausea pahoinvointi

near lähellä
nearby lähistöllä
near-sighted likinäköinen
neck kaula
necklace kaulakoru
need *v* tarvita
needle neula
nerve hermo
never ei koskaan
new uusi
newspaper sanomalehti
newsstand lehtikioski
next seuraava
next to vieressä
nice (beautiful) kaunis
night yö
no ei
noisy meluisa
none ei yhtään
non-smoking savuton
noon keskipäivä
normal normaali
north pohjoinen
nose nenä
not ei
note (bank note) seteli
notebook muistikirja
nothing ei mitään
notice (sign) varoitus
notify ilmoittaa
novice aloittelija
now nyt
number numero
nurse sairaanhoitaja

O

o'clock kello
occupation ammatti
occupied varattu
office toimisto
off-licence [BE] viinakauppa; Alko (the chain in Finland)
oil öljy

old vanha
old town vanha kaupunki
on päällä, päälle
on time aikataulussa
once kerran
one-way ticket menolippu
only vain
open adj; *v* auki; avata
opera oopera
operation toimenpide; leikkaus (medical)
operator käyttäjä (machine); operaattori (phone, internet)
opposite vastapäätä
optician optikko
or tai
orange (color) oranssi
orchestra orkesteri
order *n*; *v* tilaus; tilata
out of order epäkunnossa
out of stock loppu varastosta
outlet (electric) sähköpistorasia
outside ulkopuolella
oval soikea
overlook *n* unohdus
oxygen treatment happihoito

P

pacifier (baby's) tutti
packet paketti
pad (sanitary) terveysside
pail sanko
pain kipu
painkiller särkylääke
paint *n*; *v* maali; maalata
painting maalaus
pair pari
pajamas pyjama
palace palatsi

palpitations sydämentykytys
pants housut
panty hose sukkahousut
paper paperi
paper towel talouspaperi
parcel [BE] paketti
parents vanhemmat
park *n*; *v* puisto; pysäköidä
parking pysäköinti
parking disc pysäköintikiekko
parking garage pysäköintitalo
parking lot pysäköintialue
parking meter pysäköintimittari
part osa
part-time osa-aikainen
party (social gathering) juhlat
passport passi
passport control passintarkastus
passport photo passikuva
paste (glue) liima
pastry shop konditoria
patch paikata
path polku
patient potilas (medical); kärsivällinen (adjective)
pattern kaava
pay maksaa
payment maksu
peak *n* (mountain) huippu
pearl helmi
pedestrian jalankulkija
pediatrician lastenlääkäri
pedicure pedikyyri

peg (tent) telttakiila
pen; kynä
pencil lyijykynä
pendant riipus
penicillin penisilliini
per day päivältä
per hour tunnilta
per person hengeltä
per week viikolta
percentage
  prosentti(osuus)
perfume hajuvesi
perhaps ehkä
period (monthly)
  kuukautiset
permit n **(fishing);**
  (hunting) (kalastus)
  lupa; (metsästys)lupa
person henkilö
personal henkilökoh-
  tainen
petite pienikokoinen
petrol [BE] bensiini
pewter tina
pharmacy apteekki
phone card puhelinkortti
photo valokuva
photocopy n valokopio
photograph n valokuva
photography valokuvaus
phrase fraasi
pick up v **(go get)** hakea
picnic piknik
picnic basket eväskori
piece osa, kappale, pala
pill pilleri
pillow tyyny
PIN PIN-koodi
pin n **(brooch)** rintaneula
pink vaaleanpunainen
  (light pink); pinkki
  (bright pink)
pipe piippu
place n paikka
plane fly lentokone

planetarium planetaario
plaster [BE] (bandage)
  laastari
plastic muovi
plastic bag muovipussi
plastic wrap muo-
  vikelmu
plate lautanen
platform [BE] (station)
  laituri
platinum platina
play n **(theatre);** v
  näytelmä; leikkiä
  (child), pelata **(sport,**
  game), soittaa **(mu-**
  sic), esittää **(act)**
playground leikkikenttä
playpen leikkikehä
please ole hyvä
plug (electric) pistoke
plunger imukuppi
pneumonia keuhkokuume
pocket tasku
point of interest
  nähtävyys
point v osoittaa
poison myrkky
poisoning myrkytys
pole (ski); (tent) sauva;
  kaari
police poliisi
police report rikosilmoitus
police station
  poliisiasema
pond lampi
pool uima-allas
porcelain posliini
port satama
portable kannettava
porter kantaja
portion annos
post [BE] n; v posti;
  postittaa
post office postitoimisto

postage postimaksu
postage stamp
  postimerkki
postcard postikortti
pot purkki
pottery savenvalanta
pound (British cur-
  rency, weight) punta;
  pauna
powder puuteri
pregnant raskaana
premium (gas/petrol)
  korkeaoktaaninen
prescribe määrätä
prescription resepti
present n lahja
press (iron) prässätä
pressure paine
pretty sievä
price hinta
price-fixed menu
  kiinteähintainen
  ruokalista
print n **(photo);** v
  (document) vedos;
  tulostaa **(printer),**
  painaa **(press)**
private yksityinen
profit n voitto
program (of events)
  ohjelma
pronounce v ääntää
pronunciation n
  ääntämys
provide järjestää,
  hankkia
pull v vetää
pump pumppu
puncture puhkaista
purchase n; v ostos;
  ostaa
pure puhdas
purple purppuranpunainen
purse (handbag)
  käsilaukku

push v työntää
pushchair [BE]
  lastenrattaat
put panna

Q

quality laatu
quantity määrä
question n kysymys
quick nopea(sti)
quiet hiljainen

R

race kilpailu
race track kilparata
racket (sport) maila
radio radio
railway station [BE]
  rautatieasema
rain sade
raincoat sadetakki
rape n raiskaus
rash ihottuma
rate v **(exchange);**
  (price) kurssi; hinta,
  taksa
razor partakone
razor blade partaterä
ready valmis
real (genuine) aito
rear takana
receipt kuitti
reception vastaanotto
receptionist vastaanottovirkailija
recommend suositella
rectangular suorakul-
  mainen
red punainen
reduction vähennys
refrigerator jääkaappi
refund n v palauttaa
  maksu
regards terveiset
region alue

registered mail kirjattu lähetys

registration kirjoittautuminen

regular (gas /petrol) matalaoktaaninen

relationship suhde

reliable luotettava

religion uskonto

rent v vuokrata

rental vuokra-

rental car vuokra-auto

repair n; v korjaus; korjata

repeat v toistaa

report (theft) tehdä ilmoitus

request n; v pyyntö; pyytää

required vaadittu

requirement vaatimus

reservation varaus

reservations office varaustoimisto

reserve varata

reserved varattu

rest n lepo

restaurant ravintola

restroom WC

retired eläkkeellä

return (come back); (give back) palata; palauttaa

return ticket [BE] menopaluulippu

rib kylkiluu

ribbon nauha

right (correct); (direction) oikea

ring (jewelry); (bell) sormus; soittaa

river joki

road tie

road assistance tiepalvelu

road map tiekartta

road sign liikennemerkki

robbery ryöstö

romantic romanttinen

room (hotel); (space) huone; tila

room number huonenumero

room service huonepalvelu

room temperature huoneenlämpö

rope köysi

round pyöreä

round (golf) kierros

round-trip ticket menopaluulippu

route reitti

rowboat soutuvene

rubber (material) kumi

rubbish [BE] roska

ruby rubiini

S

safe n (vault); (not in danger); tallelokero; turvallinen

safety pin hakaneula

sailboat purjedusvene

sale n; (bargains) myynti; alennusmyynti

same sama(nlainen)

sand hiekka

sandal sandaali

sanitary napkin terveysside

sapphire safiiri

satin satiini

saucepan kattila

saucer asetti

sauna sauna

save v tallentaa (for record), säästää (not spend)

savings account

säästötili

scarf huivi

scenery maisema

scenic route maisemareitti

school koulu

scissors sakset

scooter skootteri

Scotland Skotlanti

screwdriver ruuvimeisseli

sculpture veistos

sea meri

season (year), (tourism) vuodenaika (year), sesonki (tourism)

seat istuin(paikka)

seat belt turvavyö

second (2nd), (time) toinen (2nd), sekunti (time)

second class toinen luokka

second-hand shop käytetyn tavaran kauppa

section osio

see katso

sell myydä

send lähettää

senior citizen ikäihminen

sentence lause

separated (relationship) asumuserossa

serious vakava

serve (meal) tarjoilla

service (restaurant) kattaus

set menu vakiolista

sew ommella

shampoo šampoo

shape muotoilla

sharp (pain) terävä (kipu)

shave n parranajo

shaving brush partasuti

shaving cream

partavaahto

shelf hylly

ship n v laiva; lähettää

shirt paita

shoe kenkä

shoe store kenkäkauppa

shop n kauppa, myymälä

shopping ostosten teko

shopping area ostosalue

shopping centre [BE] ostoskeskus

shopping mall ostoskeskus

short lyhyt

shorts šortsit

short-sighted [BE] likinäköinen

shoulder olkapää

shovel n lapio

show n; v esitys; esittää

shower (stall) suihku(koppi)

shrine pyhäkkö

shut kiinni

shutter (window) ikkunaluukku

side sivu (inanimate), kylki (animate)

sightseeing kiertoajelu

sightseeing tour nähtävyyskierros

sign viitta, merkki, kyltti

sign (notice) v ilmoittaa

signature allekirjoitus

silk silkki

silver hopea

silverware pöytähopeat

since alkaen

sing laulaa

single (ticket); (unmarried) meno, kertalippu; sinkku, naimaton

single room yhden hengen huone

size; (clothes); (shoes) koko

skate v luistella

skating rink luistinrata

skin iho

skirt hame

sky taivas

sleep v nukkua

sleeping bag makuupussi

sleeping car makuu-vaunu

sleeping pill unilääke

sleeve hiha

slice n pala, siivu

slide (photo) dia

slipper tohveli

slow hidas

small pieni

smoke savu

smoker tupakoitsija

snack välipala

snack bar välipalabaari

sneaker lenkkitossu

snorkeling equipment snorklausvälineet

snow lumi

soap saippua

soccer jalkapallo

soccer match jalkapallo-ottelu

sock sukka

socket (electric) sähköpistorasia

soft pehmeä

sold out loppuunmyyty

someone joku

something jotain

song laulu

soon pian

sore (painful) arka

sore throat kurkkukipu

sorry anteeksi, pahoillaan

sort (kind) laatu

south etelä

souvenir matkamuisto

souvenir shop matka-muistomyymälä

spa kylpylä

spatula lasta

speak v puhua

special erityis-

specialist erikoislääkäri

speciality erikoisuus

spell v tavuttaa

spend kuluttaa

spine selkäranka

sponge pesusieni

spoon lusikka

sport urheilulaji

sporting goods store urheiluvälinekauppa

sprained venähtänyt, nyrjähtänyt

square (shape) neliö

stadium stadion

staff henkilökunta

stain tahra

stainless steel ruostumaton teräs

stairs trappe portaat

stamp n (postage); v (ticket) postimerkki; leimata

staple niitti

star tähti

start alkaa, lähtö

starter [BE] (meal) alkuruoka

station (train); (subway) juna-asema; metroasema

stationery store paperikauppa

stay (trip); v (remain); v (reside) yöpyä; jäädä; asua

steal varastaa

sterling silver sterlinghopea

sting n; v pistos; pistää

stockings sukat

stomach maha

stomachache mahakipu

stop (bus); v stop pysäkki; pysähtyä (self), pysäyttää (other)

store (shop) kauppa, myymälä

store directory myymäläluettelo

stove hella

straight ahead suoraan eteenpäin

strange outo

street katu

street map kaupungin kartta

string naru

stroller lastenrattaat

strong vahva

student opiskelija

study v opiskella

stunning tyrmäävä

sturdy tanakka

subway metro

subway map metrokartta

suit (man's); (woman's) puku

suitcase matkalaukku

sun aurinko

sunburn auringonpolt-tama

sunglasses aurinkolasit

sunstroke auringonpistos

sun-tan lotion aurinkovoide

super (gas/petrol) korkeaoktaaninen

supermarket valinta-myymälä

supplement n liite

suppository peräpuikko

surgery [BE] lääkärin vastaanotto

surname sukunimi

swallow niellä

sweater neulepusero

sweatshirt college-pusero

sweet makea

swell turvota

swelling turvotus

swim v uida

swimming uima-

swimming pool uima-allas

swimming trunks uimahousut

swollen turvoksissa

symbol symboli

synagogue synagoga

synthetic keinotekoinen

system järjestelmä

T

table pöytä

tablet (medical) tabletti

tailor räätäli

take ottaa

take away v [BE] ottaa mukaan

taken (occupied) varattu

tampon tamponi

tap (water) vesihana

tax vero

taxi taksi

taxi rank [BE] taksitolppa

taxi stand taksitolppa

team joukkue

tear v repiä, revähdyttää

teaspoon teelusikka

telephone booth puhelinkioski

telephone directory puhelinluettelo

telephone n; v puhelin; soittaa (puhelimella)

telephone number

puhelinnumero

tell kertoa

temperature lämpötila

temple temppeli

temporary väliaikainen

tennis court tenniskenttä

tennis match tennisottelu

tennis racket tennismaila

tent teltta

tent peg telttakiila

tent pole telttakaari

terminal terminaali

terrace terassi

terrible kamala

terrifying kauhistuttava

thank kiittää

thank you kiitos

theater teatteri

theft varkaus

then sitten

there tuolla

thermometer lämpömittari

thief varas

thigh reisi

thin ohut **(material)**, laiha **(skinny)**

think (believe) uskoa, luulla

thirsty janoinen

thread lanka

throat kurkku

through läpi

thumb peukalo

thunder ukkonen

thunderstorm ukkosmyrsky

ticket lippu

ticket office lipputoimisto

tide vuorovesi

tie solmio

tie clip solmioneula

time *n*; **(recurrent oc-**

cion) aika; kerta

timetable [BE] aikataulu

tin [BE] (container) tölkki

tin opener [BE] tölkinavaaja

tire rengas

tired väsynyt

tissue nenäliina

to luokse

tobacco tupakka

tobacconist tupakkakauppa

today tänään

toe varvas

toilet [BE] WC

toilet paper WC-paperi

toiletry hygieniatuote

tomb hauta

tomorrow huomenna

tongue kieli

tonight tänä iltana

too (also) myös

too much liiaksi

tool työkalu

tooth hammas

toothache hammassärky

toothbrush hammasharja

toothpaste hammastahna

torn (clothes) revennyt

touch *v* koskettaa

tour kierros

tourist office matkailutoimisto

tow truck hinausauto

towards kohti

towel pyyhe

tower torni

town kaupunki

town hall kaupungintalo

toy lelu

toy store lelukauppa

track (train) raide

traffic light liikennevalo

trail polku

trailer asuntovaunu

train juna

tram raitiovaunu

tranquillizer rauhoittava lääke

transfer (money) siirtää rahaa

translate kääntää

travel matkustaa

travel agency matkatoimisto

travel guide matkaopas

travel sickness matkapahoinvointi

traveler's check matkašekki

treatment hoito

tree puu

trim siistiä

trip retki, matka

trolley (työntö)kärry

trousers [BE] housut

T-shirt t-paita

tube putkilo

turn (change direction) kääntyä

turtleneck poolopusero

TV TV

tweezers pinsetit

U

ugly ruma

umbrella; (beach) sateenvarjo; aurinkovarjo

unconscious tajuton

under alla, alle

underground station [BE] metroasema

underpants alushousut

undershirt aluspaita

understand ymmärtää

undress riisua

United States Yhdysvallat

university yliopisto

unleaded (fuel) lyijytön

until asti

up ylös, ylhäällä

upstairs yläkerta

urgent kiireellinen

use käyttää

usually yleensä

V

vacancy vapaa huone

vacant vapaa

vacation loma

vaccinate rokottaa

vacuum cleaner pölynimuri

valley laakso

value arvo

value-added tax [BE] arvonlisävero

vegetarian kasvissyöjä

vein suoni

very erittäin

veterinarian eläinlääkäri

video camera videokamera

view (panorama) näköala

village kylä

visit *n*; *v* vierailu; vierailla

visiting hours vierailuajat

visually impaired näkövammainen

V-neck V-aukko

volleyball game lentopallo-ottelu

voltage jännite

vomit *v* oksentaa

W

wait *v* odottaa

waiter tarjoilija

waiting room odotushuone

waitress tarjoilija
wake herätä (self);
  herättää **(other)**
wake-up call herätys-
  soitto
Wales Wales
walk n kävely
wall seinä **(indoors),**
  muuri **(outdoors)**
wallet lompakko
want haluta
warm (temperature);
  v **(reheat)** lämmin;
  lämmittää
wash pestä
washing machine
  pesukone
watch n rannekello
water vesi
waterfall vesiputous
waterproof vedenk-
  estävä
water-ski vesisukset

wave n aalto
way tie
weather sää
weather forecast
  sääennuste
week viikko
weekend viikonloppu
well kaivo **(source of
  water),** hyvin **(in a
  good way)**
west länsi
what mitä
wheel pyörä
wheelchair pyörätuoli
when milloin
where missä
which kumpi
white valkoinen
who kuka
whole kokonainen
why miksi
wide leveä
widow (female);

(male) leski
wife vaimo
wind tuuli
window; (shop) ikkuna;
  näyteikkuna
window seat ikkuna-
  paikka
windsurfer purjelautailija
wine list viinilista
wireless langaton
wish v toivoa
with kanssa
withdraw (banking) otto
without ilman
woman nainen
wonderful ihana
wood puu **(material),**
  metsä **(forest)**
wool villa
word sana
work v työskennellä,
  toimia
worse huonompi

wound haava
write kirjoittaa
wrong väärä

X

X-ray röntgen

Y

yacht huvipursi
year vuosi
yellow keltainen
yes kyllä
yesterday eilen
yet vielä
young nuori
youth hostel nuoriso-
  hostelli

Z

zero nolla
zip(per) vetoketju
zoo eläintarha
zucchini kesäkurpitsa

FINNISH – ENGLISH

A

aaakkoset alphabet
aalto wave n
aamiainen breakfast
aamu morning
aika; kerta time n;
  (recurrent occasion)
aikainen, aikaisin early
aikakauslehti magazine
aikana during
aikataulu timetable [BE]
aikataulussa on time
aito genuine
aito real (genuine)
ajaa drive ;
ajokortti driver's license

ajokortti license (driving)
ajovalo headlight
akku, paristo battery
akupunktio acupuncture
alanumero extension
  (phone)
alaosa bottom
alennus discount
alhaalla, alas down
alkaa begin
alkaa, lähtö start
alkaen since
alkoholi alcohol
alkoholi- alcoholic adj
alkuruoka starter [BE]
  (meal)

alla, alle below
alla, alle under
allekirjoitus signature
allerginen allergic
allerginen reaktio
  allergic reaction
aloittelija novice
alue district (of town)
alue region
alushousut underpants
aluspaita undershirt
ambulanssi ambulance
amerikkalainen
  American
ametisti amethyst
ammatti occupation

ämpäri bucket
annos portion
antaa give
anteeksi, pahoillaan
  sorry
antibiootti antibiotic
antiikki antique
antiikkiliike antiques
  store
antiseptinen voide
  antiseptic cream
aperitiivi aperitif
apteekki chemist [BE]
apteekki drugstore
apteekki pharmacy
apu assistance

arka sore (painful)
arkkitehti architect
aromaterapia aroma-
therapy
arvio; arvioida estimate
n; (quotation)
arvo value
arvonlisävero value-
added tax [BE]
asetti saucer
aspiriini aspirin
aste degree (temperature)
asti until
astianpesuaine dish-
washing detergent
astianpesukone
dishwasher
astiat crockery [BE]
astiat dishes (plates)
astma asthma
asumuserossa sepa-
rated (relationship)
asunto apartment
asunto flat [BE] (apartment)
asuntovaunu trailer
asuste accessory
ateria meal
aterimet flatware
auki; avata open adj; *v*
auringonpistos
sunstroke
auringonpolttama
sunburn
aurinko sun
aurinkolasit sunglasses
aurinkovoide sun-tan
lotion
Australia Australia
auto car
autonvuokraus car
hire [BE]
autonvuokraus car
rental
autotalli, korjaamo

garage
auttaa; ottaa help;
(oneself)
avain key
avainkortti key card
aviomies husband

Ä

ääniopas audio guide
ääntää pronounce *v*
ääntämys pronuncia-
tion *n*

B

baari bar
baletti ballet ballet
beige beige
bensiini gasoline
bensiini petrol [BE]
bikini bikini
britti British (person)
business-luokka busi-
ness class
butaani, nestekaasu
butane gas

C

CD-levy CD
college-pusero
sweatshirt

D

deodorantti deodorant
desinfiointiaine
disinfectant
dia slide (photo)
diabeetikko diabetic
dieselöljy diesel
digitaalinen digital
dollari dollar (U.S.)

E

e-lippu e-ticket
economy-luokka
economy class

ehkä perhaps
ehkäisyväline contra-
ceptive
ei no
ei not
ei koskaan never
ei mitään nothing
ei yhtään none
eilen yesterday
elää (to be alive), **asua**
(to stay) live *v*
eläin animal
eläinlääkäri veterinarian
eläintarha zoo
eläkkeellä retired
elastinen elastic
elektroninen electronic
elokuva movie
elokuvateatteri cinema
[BE]
emali enamel
**englannin kieli; eng-
lantilainen** English
(language); (person)
Englanti England
ennen before (time)
ennuste forecast
ensiapupakkaus
first-aid kit
ensimmäinen first
ensimmäinen luokka
first class
ensimmäinen ruokalaji
first course
**ensimmäisen
kerroksen huone**
ground-floor room [BE]
epäkunnossa out of
order
erikoislääkäri specialist
erikoisuus speciality
eritelty lasku item-
ized bill
erittäin very
erityis- special

eronnut divorced
esitellä introduce
esittely introduction
(social)
esitys; esittää show *n; v*
etelä south
etiketti label
Euroopan unioni
European Union
Eurooppa Europe
eväskori picnic basket

F

faksi fax
faksinumero fax number
farkkukangas denim
farkut jeans
filmi film [BE]
flunssa flu
föönaus blow dry
fraasi phrase

G

galleria gallery
golfkenttä golf course
golfmaila golf club
golfturnaus golf
tournament
gramma gram
grillihiili charcoal
gynekologi gynecologist

H

haarukka fork
haava wound
haava; leikata cut
n (wound); *v* (with
scissors)
häiritä bother
häiritä disturb
hajuvesi perfume
hakaneula safety pin
hakea pick up *v* (go get)
halata halpa cheap
haluta want

hame skirt
hammas tooth
hammasharja toothbrush
hammaslääkäri dentist
hammasproteesi denture
hammassärky toothache
hammastahna toothpaste
hämmästyttävä amazing
hansikas glove
happihoito oxygen treatment
harja brush *n*
harmaa gray
harva few
hätä emergency
hätäuloskäynti emergency exit
hattu hat
hauta tomb
hautausmaa cemetery
hehkulamppu light bulb
hei hello
hei hi
heinänuha hay fever
hella stove
helmi pearl
helppo easy
hengeltä per person
hengenpelastaja life guard (beach)
hengittää breathe
henkilö person
henkilökohtainen personal
henkilökunta staff
henkilöllisyystodistus identification (card)
herätä (self); **herättää** (other) wake
herätyskello alarm clock
herätyssoitto wake-up call

herkkumyymälä delicatessen
herkullinen delicious
hermo nerve
herra Mr.
hetki moment
hidas slow
hiekka sand
hieno great (excellent)
hieronta massage
hiha sleeve
hiljainen quiet
hinausauto tow truck
hinta price
hiottu lasi cut glass
hissi elevator
hissi lift [BE] elevator
historia history
hiukset hair
hiusharja hairbrush
hiuskiinne hairspray
hiustenkuivain hair dryer
hoito treatment
hopea silver
hotelli hotel
hotellin varaus hotel reservation
hotelliopas hotel directory
housut pants
housut trousers [BE]
huimaantunut dizzy
huippu peak *n* (mountain)
huivi scarf
huokea inexpensive
huomenna tomorrow
huone; tila room (hotel); (space)
huoneen luovutus check out *v*
huoneenlämpö room temperature
huonekalut furniture
huonenumero room number

huonepalvelu room service
huono, kehno bad
huonompi worse
huuli lip
huulipuna lipstick
huvipuisto amusement park
huvipursi yacht
hygieniatuote toiletry
hylly shelf
hyökkäys attack *n*
hyönteisen pisto insect bite
hyönteismyrkky insect repellent
hyönteissuihke insect spray
hytti cabin (ship)
hyttysverkko mosquito net
hyvä good
hyvää huomenta good morning
hyvää iltaa good evening
hyvää iltapäivää good afternoon
hyvää yötä good night
hyväksyä accept *v* (approval)
hyvästi goodbye
hyvin, hyvä fine (OK)

I

ihana lovely
ihana wonderful
iho skin
ihottuma rash
ikä age
ikäihminen senior citizen
ikävystyttävä boring
ikkuna; näyteikkuna window; (shop)
ikkunaluukku shutter (window)

ikkunapaikka window seat
ilmainen (of charge), **vapaa** (not restricted) free
ilmaisu expression
ilman without
ilmapatja air mattress
ilmastointi air conditioning
ilmoittaa notify
ilmoittaa sign (notice) *v*
iloinen, onnellinen happy
ilta evening
iltapäivä afternoon
imukuppi plunger
internet internet
internetkahvila internet cafe
Irlanti Ireland
irlantilainen Irish (person); adj
irrottaa disconnect *v* (computer)
Iso-Britannia Great Britain
istuin(paikka) seat
itä east
itsepalvelupesula launderette [BE]
itsepalvelupesula laundromat

J

ja and
jää ice
jäädä pois get off
jääkaappi refrigerator
jäinen icy (weather)
jakku jacket
jalankulkija pedestrian
jalka foot
jalka leg
jalkapallo football [BE]

jalkapallo soccer
jalkapallo-ottelu soccer match
jälkeen after
jälkiruoka dessert
jalokivi gem
jänis hare
jännite voltage
janoinen thirsty
järjestää, hankkia provide
järjestelmä system
jarru brake *n*
järvi lake
jazz jazz
jodi iodine
johtaja manager
joka each
joka every
joki river
joku someone
jos if
jossain, missään anywhere
jotain something
joukkue team
juhlat party (social gathering)
juna train
juna-asema; metroasema station (train); (subway)
juoma; juoda drink *n*; (cocktail); *v*
juomavesi drinking water
jyrkänne cliff

K

kaamea awful
kääntää translate
kääntyä turn (change direction)
kaasu gas
kaatua fall *v*
kaava pattern

kaavake form (document)
kahden hengen huone double room
kahvila cafe
kaihdin blind (window)
kaikki everything
kaivo (source of water), **hyvin** (in a good way) well
kalastus fishing
kalenteri calendar
kallis expensive
kalvosinnappi cufflink
kamala terrible
kamera camera
kameralaukku camera case
kampa comb
kampaaja hairdresser
Kanada Canada
kanadalainen Canadian
kangas cloth
kangas fabric (cloth)
kannettava portable
kansainvälinen lento international flight
kansallisuus nationality
kansi deck (ship)
kansituoli deck chair
kanssa with
kantaa carry
kantaja porter
kapea narrow
karahvi carafe
kartonki carton (of cigarettes)
kartta map
käsi hand
käsilaukku handbag [BE]
käsilaukku purse (handbag)
käsin tehty handmade
kasino casino
käsinpestävä hand washable

käsityö(tuotteet) handicrafts
käsivarsi arm
käsivoide hand cream
kassa cashier
kasvissyöjä vegetarian
kasvitiede botany
kasvitieteellinen puutarha botanical garden
kasvohoito facial
kasvot face
kasvovesi astringent
katso see
katsoa look *v*
kattaus service (restaurant)
kattila saucepan
katu street
kauhistuttava terrifying
kaukana far
kaukonäköinen farsighted
kaukonäköinen longsighted [BE]
kaula neck
kaulakoru necklace
kaulus collar
kauneushoitola beauty salon
kaunis beautiful
kaunis nice (beautiful)
kauppa, myymälä shop *n*
kauppa, myymälä store (shop)
kaupungin kartta street map
kaupungin keskusta center of town
kaupungintalo town hall
kaupunki town
(työntö)kärry baggage check
(työntö)kärry cart
(työntö)kärry luggage

cart
(työntö)kärry trolley
kävely walk *n*
käyntikortti business card
käytäväpaikka aisle seat
käytetyn tavaran kauppa second-hand shop
käyttää use
käyttäjä (machine); **operaattori** (phone, internet) operator
käyttötili checking account
kehykset frame (glasses)
keinotekoinen synthetic
keittiö cuisine
keittiömestari chef
kello clock
kello o'clock
keltainen yellow
kemiallinen WC chemical toilet
kenkä shoe
kenkäkauppa shoe store
keramiikka ceramics
kerosiini kerosene
kerran once
kertoa tell
kesäkurpitsa zucchini
keski- middle
keskinkertainen average
keskipäivä noon
keskiyö midnight
keskusta-alue downtown area
keuhko lung
keuhkokuume pneumonia
kieli language
kieli tongue
kielletty forbidden
kierros round (golf)
kierros tour

kiertoajelu sightseeing
kiertotie detour (traffic)
kiikari binoculars
kiinni shut
kiinnostunut interested
kiinteähintainen
   ruokalista price-fixed
   menu
kiireellinen urgent
kiirehtiä hurry
kiireinen busy
kiitos thank you
kiittää thank
kilogramma kilogram
kilometri kilometer
kilometrimäärä mileage
kilpailu race
kilparata race track
kippis cheers
kipu pain
kipua lievittävä
   analgesic
kirja book
kirjailu embroidery
kirjakauppa bookstore
kirjasto library
kirjattu lähetys
   registered mail
kirjautua sisään log on
kirjautua sisään login
kirjautua ulos log off
kirje (message), kirjain
   (of the alphabet) letter
kirjekuori envelope
kirjoittaa write
kirjoittautuminen
   registration
kirkko church
kirpputori flea market
klassinen classical
kodinkone appliance
kohdalla at
kohti towards
koira dog
koko size; (clothes);
(shoes)
kokoaikainen full-time
kokonainen whole
kokoushuone confer-
   ence room
kokoussali convention
   hall
kolikko coin
komedia comedy
kompassi compass
konditoria pastry shop
kondomi condom
konerikko breakdown
   (car)
konsertti concert
konserttisali concert hall
konsulaatti consulate
koputtaa knock
kori basket
koripallo-ottelu
   basketball game
(auton)korjaaja car
   mechanic
korjata alter v
korjata mend
korjata, paikata fix v
korjaus; korjata
   repair n; v
korkea high adj
korkea vuorovesi
   high tide
korkeaoktaaninen
   premium (gas/petrol)
korkeaoktaaninen
   super (gas/petrol)
korkkiruuvi corkscrew
korko interest (finance)
kortti card
korttipeli card game
korva ear
korvakoru earring
korvasärky earache
korvatipat ear drops
koskettaa touch v
kosteusemulsio lotion

kosteuspyyhkeet baby
   wipes
kosteusvoide moistur-
   izing cream
koti home
kotimaa domestic
   (airport terminal)
kotimaanlento domestic
   flight
koulu school
kova hard
kova loud (voice)
köysi rope
kristalli crystal
kruunu crown (Danish
   currency)
kuinka how
kuinka kauan how long
kuinka kaukana how far
kuinka monta how many
kuinka paljon how much
kuitti receipt
kuiva dry
kuivapesula dry cleaner
kuka who
kukaan anyone
kukka flower
kukkakauppias florist
kulho bowl
kulma corner
kulta gold
kultasepänliike jeweler
kulu expense
kuluttaa spend
kumi rubber (material)
kumpi which
kuntosali gym
kupari copper
kuppi cup
kurkku throat
kurkkukipu sore throat
kurssi; hinta, taksa rate
   n (exchange); (price)
kutsu invitation
kutsua invite v

kuu moon
kuukausi month
kuukautiset period
   (monthly)
kuukautiskivut cramps
kuulokkeet headphones
kuulovammainen
   hearing-impaired
kuuma hot (temperature)
kuume fever
kuunnella listen
kylä village
kylkiluu rib
kyllä yes
kylpy bath
kylpyhuone bathroom
kylpylä spa
kylpytakki bathrobe
kynä pen
kynsi nail (body)
kynsihoitola nail salon
kynsileikkuri nail
   clippers
kynsiviila nail file
kynttilä candle
kypärä helmet
kysymys question n
kyvykäs able

L

lääkäri doctor
lääkärin vastaanotto
   doctor's office
lääkärin vastaanotto
   surgery [BE]
lääkärintarkastus
   check-up (medical)
lääke medicine (drug)
laakso valley
laastari plaster [BE]
   (bandage)
laatikko box
laatu quality
laatu sort (kind)
lähde fountain

lähellä near
lähettää send
lähistöllä nearby
lahja gift
lahja present *n*
lahjatavarakauppa gift shop
lähteä depart
lähteä; jättää leave *v*; (behind)
lähtö departure
lähtöportti departure gate
lähtöselvitys check-in desk (airport)
lähtöselvitys e-lipulla e-ticket check-in
laituri platform (BE) (station)
laiva; lähettää ship *n v*
lakimies lawyer
lakki cap
laktoosi-intolerantikko lactose intolerant
lämmin; lämmittää warm (temperature); *v* (reheat)
lämmittää heat *v*
lämmitys heating
lampi pond
lämpömittari thermometer
lämpötila temperature
lamppu lamp
langaton wireless
lanka thread
länsi west
läpi through
lapio shovel *n*
lapsen sänky cot
lapsenvahti babysitter
lapsi child barn
lasi glass (drinking)
laskin calculator
lasku invoice

lasku; šekki; tarkistaa check (restaurant) n; (banking); *v* (someone, something)
lasku; seteli bill (restaurant); (bank note)
lasta spatula
lastenallas kiddie pool
lastenannos children's portion
lastenistuin child's seat
lastenlääkäri pediatrician
lastenlapsi grandchild
lastenrattaat pushchair [BE]
lastenrattaat stroller
lastenvaatteet children's clothing
lattia (of a room), **kerros** (of a building) floor
(kamera)laukku case (camera)
laukku; kassi bag (purse/ handbag); (shopping)
laulaa sing
laulu song
lause sentence
lautanen plate
lautasliina napkin
lautta ferry
lehtikioski newsstand
leikkikehä playpen
leikkikenttä playground
leipomo bakery
leirintä camping
leirintäpaikka campsite
leirintävarusteet camping equipment
leirintävuode camp bed
leiriytyä camp *v*
lelu toy
lelukauppa toy store
leninki, mekko dress *n*
lenkkitossu sneaker

lento flight
lentokenttä, lentoasema airport
lentokone airplane
lentokone plane fly
lentopallo-ottelu volleyball game
lentoposti airmail
lepo rest *n*
leski widow (female); (male)
leuka jaw
leveä wide
lihakauppa butcher
lihas muscle
liiaksi too much
liikekeskus business district
liikematka business trip
liikennemerkki road sign
liikennevalo traffic light
liiketoimintakeskus business center (at hotel)
liikkua (self), **liikuttaa** (other) move *v*
liima glue
liima paste (glue)
liite supplement *n*
liitin clip
liittää join *v*
likainen dirty
likinäköinen nearsighted
likinäköinen shortsighted [BE]
linja-auto bus
linja-autoasema bus station
linja-autopysäkki bus stop
linna castle slot;
linssi lens (camera); (glasses)

lintu bird
lippu ticket
lipputoimisto ticket office
lippuvihko booklet (of tickets)
lisä extra
lisää more
litra liter
loma vacation
lompakko wallet
loppu end
loppu varastosta out of stock
loppuunmyyty sold out
louferit loafers
loukata hurt
loukata injure
lounas lunch
löytää find *v*
löytötavaratoimisto lost and found
löytötavaratoimisto lost property office [BE]
luistella skate *v*
luistinrata skating rink
lumi snow
lunastaa; käteinen cash *v; n*
luokse to
luola cave
luomiväri eye shadow
luonnollinen natural
luontaistuotemyymälä health food store
luotettava reliable
(kalastus)lupa; (metsästys)lupa permit *n* (fishing); (hunting)
luottokortti credit card
lusikka spoon
luu bone
luuta broom

lyhty lantern
lyhyt short
lyijykynä pencil
lyijytön unleaded (fuel)

M

maa country
maahantuotu imported
maalaus painting
maali; maalata paint n; v
määrä quantity
määrätä prescribe
maaseutu countryside
maatila farm
maha stomach
mahakipu stomachache
maila racket (sport)
maisema landscape
maisema scenery
maisemareitti scenic route
majatalo inn
makea sweet
makeiskauppa candy store
mäki hill
maksaa pay
maksu fare (ticket)
maksu payment
maksu; maksaa cost n; v
maksu; veloittaa charge n; v
maksumääräys money order
makuupaikka, vuode-paikka berth
makuupussi sleeping bag
makuuvaunu sleeping car
manikyyri manicure
matala low
matala vuorovesi low tide
matalaoktaaninen

regular (gas /petrol)
materiaali material
matinea matinée
matka journey
matkailutoimisto tourist office
matkalaukku suitcase
matkamuisto souvenir
matkamuistomyymälä souvenir shop
matkaopas travel guide
matkapahoinvointi travel sickness
matkapuhelin cell phone
matkapuhelin mobile phone [BE]
matkašekki traveler's check
matkatavara baggage [BE]
matkatavaran nouto baggage claim
matkatavaran säilytys left-luggage office [BE]
matkatavarat luggage
matkatoimisto travel agency
matkustaa travel
matkustajakoti guesthouse
meijeri dairy
meikki make-up n
mekaaninen (adjective), **korjaaja** (person) mechanic
meluisa noisy
menetetty (forgone), **kadotettu** (misplaced) lost
menettää (forgo), **kadot-taa** (misplace) lose
menetys loss
mennä pois go away
mennä rikki break (out of order)

mennä sisään enter v
mennä takaisin go back
mennä ulos (literally), **sammua** (of a flame) go out
meno, kertalippu; sinkku, naimaton single n (ticket); (unmarried)
menolippu one-way ticket
menopaluulippu return ticket [BE]
menopaluulippu round-trip ticket
meri sea
meripihka amber
merivirta current (ocean)
messu mass (religious service)
messut (expo), **vaalea** (light), **reilu** (just) fair
metri meter
metro subway
metroasema under-ground station [BE]
metrokartta subway map
metsä forest
metsästys hunting
mielenkiintoinen interesting
mielialalääke antide-pressant
mies man
miksi why
milloin when
minä I
minuutti minute
missä where
mitä what
mitään anything
mitata measure
mittakuppi measuring cup

mittalusikka measuring spoon
monta many
moottoripyörä motorcycle
moottoritie highway
moottoritie motorway [BE]
moottorivene motorboat
mopo moped
moppi mop n
moskeija mosque
motelli motel
muistikirja notebook
muistikortti memory card
muistomerkki memorial
muistomerkki monu-ment
muki mug n
munuainen kidney
muotoilla shape
muovi plastic
muovikelmu plastic wrap
muovipussi plastic bag
murtomaahiihto cross-country skiing
museo museum
musiikki music
musikaali musical
musta black
mustelma bruise
mutta but
myöhään; myöhässä late (time); (delay)
myös also
myös too (also)
myrkky poison
myrkytys poisoning
myydä sell
myymäläluettelo store directory
myynti; alennusmyynti sale n; (bargains)

N

nahka leather
nähtävyys point of interest
nähtävyyskierros sightseeing tour
naimisissa married
nainen woman
näkö eyesight
näköala view (panorama)
näkövammainen visually impaired
nälkäinen hungry
nappi button
naru string
nauha ribbon
nauraa laugh
näytelmä, leikkiä (child), **pelata** (sport, game), **soittaa** (music), **esittää** (act) play n (theatre); v
näyttely exhibition
neiti Miss
neliö square (shape)
nenä nose
nenäliina handkerchief
nenäliina tissue
neste fluid
neula needle
neule knitwear
neulepusero sweater
neuletakki cardigan
neuvonta information
neuvontapiste information desk
niellä swallow
niitti staple
niitty meadow
nilkka ankle
nimi name
nivel joint (anatomy)
noin about
nolla zero
nopea fast adj

nopea(sti) quick
normaali normal
nousta ylös get up
nuija mallet
nukke doll
nukkua sleep v
numero number
nuori young
nuorisohostelli youth hostel
nyrkkeilyottelu boxing match
nyt now

O

odottaa expect
odottaa wait v
odotushuone waiting room
ohjelma program (of events)
ohut (material), **laiha** (skinny) thin
oikea right (correct); (direction)
oikeustalo court house
oksentaa vomit v
ole hyvä please
öljy oil
olkapää shoulder
olla be
olla perillä, saapua, tulla arrive
olo feel (physical state)
ommella sew
onnettomuus accident
onni luck
onnittelut congratulations
ooppera opera
opas guide n
opaskirja guidebook
opaskoira guide dog
opiskelija student
opiskella study v

oppitunti lesson
optikko optician
oranssi orange (color)
orkesteri orchestra
osa part
osa-aikainen part-time
osa, kappale, pala piece
osallistua attend
osasto department (shop)
osio section
osoite address n
osoittaa point v
ostaa buy
ostos; ostaa purchase n; v
ostosalue shopping area
ostoskeskus mall
ostoskeskus shopping centre [BE]
ostoskeskus shopping mall
ostosten teko shopping
ötökkä bug
ottaa take
ottaa mukaan take away v [BE]
ottelu match n (sport)
otto withdraw (banking)
outo strange

P

pää head
päällä, päälle on on
päänsärky headache
päästää sisään admitted
pääsy access n
pääsymaksu entrance fee
päätös decision
pahoinvointi nausea
paikallinen local
paikata patch
paikka filling (tooth)
paikka place n

paine pressure
paistinpannu frying pan
paita shirt
päivä day
päivällinen dinner
päivältä per day
pakastin freezer
paketti packet
paketti parcel [BE]
pakkanen frost
pala, siivu slice n
palata; palauttaa return (come back); (give back)
palatsi palace
palauttaa maksu refund v
paljon much
palo-ovi fire door
palohaava burn
palopakotie fire escape
palouloskäynti fire exit
palvelumaksu cover charge
pankki bank (finance)
pankkiautomaatti ATM
panna put
pano; ennakkomaksu deposit n (bank); (down payment)
paperi paper
paperikauppa stationery store
parempi better
pari pair
parivuode double bed
parranajo shave n
parta beard
partakone razor
partasuti shaving brush
partaterä razor blade
partavaahto shaving cream
partavesi aftershave lotion

parturi barber
parveke balcony
passi passport
passikuva passport photo
passintarkastus passport control
patja mattress
pedikyyri pedicure
pehmeä soft
peili mirror
peitto blanket
pelastusliivi life jacket
pelastusrengas life preserver
pelastusvene life boat
peli game
pelihalli arcade
pellava linen
pelto, kenttä field
penisilliini penicillin
peräpuikko suppository
perhe family
peruuttaa cancel
pestä wash
pesuaine detergent
pesukone washing machine
pesula laundry
pesulapalvelu laundry service
pesusieni sponge
peukalo thumb
pian soon
pieni small
pienikokoinen petite
piilolinssi contact lens
piippu pipe
pika express
pikaruokapaikka fast-food place
pikaviestin instant messenger instant messenger
piknik picnic
pilleri pill

pilvi cloud
pimeä, tumma dark
PIN-koodi PIN
pinsetit tweezers
pistoke plug (electric)
pistos; pistää sting n; v
pitää keep
pitää; miellyttää like; (please)
pitkä long
pitsi lace
planetaario planetarium
platina platinum
pohjoinen north
poika boy
poikaystävä boyfriend
pois away
poliisi police
poliisiasema police station
polku path
polku trail
polvi knee
pölynimuri vacuum cleaner
poolopusero turtleneck
portaat stairs trappe
posliini porcelain
poste restante general delivery
posti; postittaa mail n; v
posti; postittaa post [BE] n; v
postikortti postcard
postilaatikko mailbox
postimaksu postage
postimerkki postage stamp
postimerkki; leimata stamp n (postage); v (ticket)
postitoimisto post office
potilas (medical); **kärsivällinen** (adj)

patient
(sisään)pääsy admission
pöytä table
pöytähopeat silverware
prässätä press (iron)
prosentti(osuus) percentage
puhdas pure
puhdas; puhdistaa clean adj; v
puhdistusvoide cleansing cream
puhelin; soittaa (puhelimella) telephone n; v
puhelinkioski telephone booth
puhelinkortti phone card
puhelinluettelo directory (phone)
puhelinluettelo telephone directory
puhelinnumero telephone number
puhelu; kutsua call n (phone); v; (summon)
puhkaista puncture
puhua speak v
puisto; pysäköidä park n; v
puku suit (man's); (woman's)
pullo bottle
pullonavaaja bottle opener
pumppu pump
punainen red
punta; pauna pound (British currency; weight)
purjehdusvene sailboat
purjelautailija windsurfer
purkki jar (container)
purkki pot

purppuranpunainen purple
pusero blouse
putkilo tube
puu tree
puu (material), **metsä** (forest) wood
puudutusaine anesthetic
puutarha garden
puuteri powder
puuttua miss v (lacking)
puuvilla cotton
pyhäkkö shrine
pyhäpäivä; loma holiday; [BE]
pyjama pajamas
(polku)pyörä bicycle
pyöräilykisa cycling race
pyöräilyreitti bike route
pyörätuoli wheelchair
pyöreä round
pysäkki; pysähtyä (self), **pysäyttää** (other) stop (bus); v stop
pysäköinti parking
pysäköintialue car park [BE]
pysäköintialue parking lot
pysäköintikiekko disc (parking)
pysäköintikiekko parking disc
pysäköintimittari parking meter
pysäköintitalo parking garage
pystyä; tölkki can v (be able to); n (container)
pyyhe towel
pyyhekumi eraser
pyyntö; pyytää request n; v

R

räätäli tailor
radio radio
raha money
raide track (train)
raiskaus rape *n*
raitiovaunu tram
rakastaa love *v*
rakennus building
rakentaa build
rakko blister
rannekello watch *n*
rannekoru bracelet
rantapallo beach ball
raskaana pregnant
raskas, painava heavy
ratsastus horseback
　riding
rauhallinen calm
rauhanen gland
rauhoittava lääke
　tranquillizer
rautakauppa hardware
　store
rautatieasema railway
　station [BE]
ravintola restaurant
ravintolavaunu
　dining car
reikä hole
reisi thigh
reitti route
rengas tire
repiä, revähdyttää tear *v*
reppu backpack
resepti prescription
retki excursion
retki, matka trip
revennyt torn (clothes)
riippumatto hammock
riipus pendant
riisua undress
rikki, murtunut broken
rikosilmoitus police
　report

rinta breast
rintakehä chest
rintakipu chest pain
rintakoru brooch
rintaliivit bra
rintaneula pin *n* (brooch)
ripuli diarrhea
(vaate)ripustin hanger
risteys intersection
rokottaa vaccinate
romanttinen romantic
röntgen X-ray
roska garbage
roska rubbish [BE]
rouva Mrs.
rubiini ruby
ruiske injection
rullaportaat escalator
ruma ugly
ruoanlaittomahdollis-
　uus cooking facilities
ruoka food
ruokalaji dish (food item)
ruokalista menu;
ruokamyrkytys food
　poisoning
ruokasali dining room
ruokavalio diet
ruostumaton teräs
　stainless steel
ruskea brown
ruumis body
ruuvimeisseli
　screwdriver
ryhmä group
ryöstö mugging
ryöstö robbery

S

sää weather
saada get (find)
sääennuste weather
　forecast
saapas boot
saapuvat arrival

säästötili savings account
saattaa may *v*
sade rain
sadetakki raincoat
safiiri sapphire
sähkö electricity
sähköinen electric
sähköpistorasia electri-
　cal outlet
sähköpistorasia outlet
　(electric)
sähköpistorasia socket
　(electric)
sähköposti e-mail
sähköpostiosoite
　e-mail address
säilytyslokero luggage
　locker
saippua soap
sairaala hospital
sairaanhoitaja nurse
sairas ill [BE]
sairaus illness
sairausvakuutus health
　insurance
šakki chess
šakkipeli chess set
sakset scissors
salama lightning
saldo balance (finance)
saldo (prepaid telephone),
　luotto (payment) credit
sali hall (room)
sama(nlainen) same
šampoo shampoo
sana word
sanakirja dictionary
sandaali sandal
sanko pail
sanomalehti newspaper
särky ache
särkylääke painkiller
satama harbor
satama port
sateenvarjo; aurinko-

varjo umbrella; (beach)
satiini satin
sauna sauna
sauva; kaari pole (ski);
　(tent)
savenvalanta pottery
savu smoke
savuke cigarette
savuton non-smoking
seinä (indoors), **muuri**
　(outdoors) wall
sekalainen assorted
sekalaiset miscellaneous
šekki cheque [BE]
selkä back
selkäranka spine
selkäsärky backache
selvittää clear *v*
senttimetri centimeter
seteli banknote
seteli note (bank note)
seuraava next
seurata follow
side bandage *n*
sideharso gauze
sievä pretty
siirtää rahaa transfer
　(money)
siistiä trim
siivooja maid
sijoitus investment
sikari cigar
silitysrauta; silittää
　iron *n* (clothing); *v*
silkki silk
silmä eye
silmälasit glasses
　(optical)
silmätipat eye drops
silta bridge
sininen blue
sisä- indoor
sisäänkäynti entrance
sisäänpääsy entry
　(access)

sisältää contain
sisältää include
sisässä, sisällä in
sisässä, sisälle inside
sitten then
sivu (inanimate), **kylki** (animate) side
skootteri scooter
Skotlanti Scotland
smaragdi emerald
snorklausvälineet snorkeling equipment
soikea oval
soittokello bell (electric)
solmio tie
solmioneula tie clip
sopimus contract
sormi finger
sormus; soittaa ring (jewelry); (bell)
šortsit shorts
soutuvene rowboat
sovitin adapter
sovittaa fit *v*
sovittu tapaaminen, aika appointment
sovituskoppi fitting room
stadion stadium
sterlinghopea sterling silver
suhde relationship
suihku(koppi) shower (stall)
sukat stockings
sukka sock
sukkahousut panty hose
sukunimi surname
suljettu closed
sulkea close *v*
summa amount *n* (money)
sumu fog
suoda anteeksi excuse *v*

suodatin filter
suoli bowel
suoni vein
suora; opastaa direct adj; *v* (someone)
suoraan eteenpäin straight ahead
suorakulmainen rectangular
suositella recommend
suu mouth
suudella kiss *v*
suunnasta from
suunnilleen around (approximately)
suunta direction
suuntaan, sijaan for
suurenmoinen magnificent
suurentaa enlarge
suuri large
suuri, iso big
suurlähetystö embassy
suuvesi mouthwash
sydämentykytys palpitations
sydän heart
sydänkohtaus heart attack
symboli symbol
synagoga synagogue
syntymä birth
syntymäpäivä birthday
syntynyt born
syödä eat
syöttää feed *v*
syöttötuoli highchair
sytytin lighter
syvä deep

T

t-paita T-shirt
täällä here
tabletti tablet (medical)
tahra stain

tähti star
tai or
taide art
taidegalleria art gallery
taistelukenttä battleground
taiteet fine arts
taivas sky
tajuton unconscious
takana rear
takana, taakse behind
takki coat *n* (clothing)
taksi taxi
taksitolppa taxi rank [BE]
taksitolppa taxi stand
tallelokero; turvallinen safe *n* (vault); (not in danger)
tallentaa (for record), **säästää** (not spend) save *v*
talo house
talouspaperi paper towel
tamponi tampon
tänä iltana tonight
tänään today
tanakka sturdy
Tanska Denmark
tanskalainen Danish (person); adj
tanssi; tanssia dance *n*; *v*
tarjoilija waiter
tarjoilija waitress
tarjoilla serve (meal)
tarkastus control
tärkeä important
tarkoittaa mean *v*
tarpeeksi enough
tarttuva contagious
tarvita need *v*
tasku pocket
taskulamppu flashlight

tauti disease
tavaratalo department store
tavata meet
tavuttaa spell *v*
täysi full
täyttää fill in (form)
täytyä must (have to)
täytyä; omistaa have (must); (possess)
teatteri theater
teelusikka teaspoon
tehdä ilmoitus report (theft)
tehdas factory
teltta tent
telttakaari tent pole
telttakiila peg (tent)
telttakiila tent peg
telttapatja groundsheet
temppeli temple
tenniskenttä tennis court
tennismaila tennis racket
tennisottelu tennis match
terä blade
terassi terrace
terävä (kipu) sharp (pain)
terminaali terminal
tervehdys greeting
terveiset regards
terveyssside pad (sanitary)
terveysside sanitary napkin
tie road
tie way
tiedustelu inquiry
tiekartta road map
tienhaara crossroads
tiepalvelu road assistance

tietää know
tietokone computer (PC)
tilaus; tilata order *n; v*
tili account
timantti diamond
tina pewter
tippa drop (liquid)
tippua drip
tiski counter
todistus certificate
tohveli slipper
toimenpide; leikkaus (medical) operation
toimisto office
toimittaa deliver
toimitus delivery
toinen (2nd), **sekunti** (time) second
toinen luokka second class
toistaa repeat *v*
toivoa wish *v*
tölkinavaaja can opener
tölkinavaaja tin opener [BE]
tölkki tin [BE] (container)
(kauppa)tori market *n*
torni tower
treffit; päivämäärä date (appointment);(day)
tukanleikkuu haircut
tukossa blocked
tullata declare (customs)
tullauslomake customs declaration form
tulli customs
tulli duty (customs)

tunnilta per hour
tunti hour (time)
tuoda bring
tuoda alas bring down
tuoli chair
tuolla there
tuore (of food), **raikas** (of air and water) fresh
tupakka tobacco
tupakkakauppa tobacconist
tupakoitsija smoker
turvaistuin car seat
turvavyö seat belt
turvoksissa swollen
turvota swell
turvotus swelling
tusina dozen
tutti dummy [BE] (baby's) [pacifier]
tuttipullo baby bottle
tuuletin fan
tuuli wind
TV TV
tyhjä empty
työkalu tool
työntää push *v*
työskennellä, toimia work *v*
työtoveri colleague
tyrmäävä stunning
tyttö girl
tyttöystävä girlfriend
tyyny pillow

U

uida swim *v*
uima- swimming
uima-allas pool
uima-allas swimming pool
uimahousut swimming trunks
uimapuku bathing suit
ukkonen thunder

ukkosmyrsky thunderstorm
ulkomaat international; (airport terminal)
ulkomainen foreign
ulkopuolella outside
uloskäynti; poistua exit *n; v* (computer)
ulostuslääke laxative
ummetus constipation
umpilisäke (anatomy) appendix
unilääke sleeping pill
unohdus overlook *n*
unohtaa forget
urheilulaji sport
urheiluvälinekauppa sporting goods store
uskoa, luulla think (believe)
uskonto religion
uudelleen again
uusi new

V

V-aukko V-neck
vaadittu required
vaalea; kevyt light (color); (weight)
vaaleanpunainen (light pink); **pinkki** (bright pink) pink
vaara danger
väärä wrong
vaarallinen dangerous
vaatekauppa clothing store
vaatimus requirement
vaatteet clothing
vaatteidenpesumahdollisuus laundry facilities
vähän little (amount)
vähemmän less
vähennys reduction

vahva strong
vahvistaa confirm
vahvistus confirmation
vaihtaa (rahaa) exchange *v* (money)
vaihtokurssi exchange rate
vaihtoraha; vaihtaa (rahaa); vaihtaa (vaatteet, vaippa) change *n* (money); *v* (money); *v* (clothes, diaper)
vaikea difficult
vaikuttava impressive
vaimo wife
vain just (only)
vain only
vaippa diaper
vaippa nappy [BE]
vakava serious
vakiolista set menu
vakuutus insurance
vakuutushakemus insurance claim
väliaikainen temporary
valinta choice
valintamyymälä supermarket
välipala snack
välipalabaari snack bar
välissä, välillä between
valitus complaint
välityspalkkio commission (fee)
välityspalkkio fee (commission)
valkaisuaine bleach
valkoinen white
valmis ready
valokopio photocopy *n*
valokuva photo
valokuva photograph *n*
valokuvaus photography

valokuvausliike camera shop

valuutanvaihto (toimisto) currency exchange office

valuutta currency

vamma injury

vammainen disabled

vanha old

vanha kaupunki old town

vanhemmat parents

vapaa vacant

vapaa huone vacancy

varas thief

varastaa steal

varata reserve

varattu engaged (phone)

varattu occupied

varattu reserved

varattu taken (occupied)

varaus reservation

varaustoimisto reservations office

väri color

värikynä crayon

värjätä dye

varkaus theft

varma certain

varoitus caution

varoitus notice (sign)

varusteet equipment

varvas toe

vasara hammer

vasen left

vastaan against

vastaanotto reception

vastaanottovirkailija receptionist

vastapäätä opposite

vastaus answer

väsynyt tired

vaunuosasto compart-

ment (train)

vaurioitunut damaged

vauva baby

vauvan sänky crib

vauvanruoka baby food

vedenkestävä waterproof

vedos; tulostaa (printer), painaa (press) print n (photo); v (document)

veistos sculpture

veitsi knife

venähtänyt, nyrjähtänyt sprained

vene, lautta, alus boat

venematka boat trip

verenpaine blood pressure

verho curtain

veri blood

vero tax

verovapaa myymälä duty-free shop

verovapaat tavarat duty-free goods

vesi water

vesihana faucet

vesihana tap (water)

vesiputous waterfall

vesiskootteri jet ski

vesisukset water-ski

vetää pull v

vetoketju zip(per)

viaton innocent

videokamera video camera

viehättävä attractive

vielä yet

vierailu; vierailla visit n; v

vierailuajat visiting hours

vieressä next to

viesti message

vihannesmyymälä greengrocer's [BE]

vihreä green

viihtyisä enjoyable

viikko week

viikolta per week

viikonloppu weekend

viikset moustache

viila file (for nails)

viimeinen last

viinakauppa; Alko (the chain in Finland) liquor store

viinakauppa; Alko (the chain in Finland) off-licence [BE]

viinilista wine list

viitta, merkki, kyltti sign

viivytys delay

villa wool

vilustuminen; kylmä cold (illness); adj

virhe mistake

virtsarakko bladder

vitriini display case

voide cream (toiletry)

voitto profit n

vuode bed

vuodenaika (year), sesonki (tourism) season

vuokra- rental

vuokra-auto rental car

vuokrata hire [BE] v

vuokrata rent v

vuoristotauti altitude sickness

vuorovesi tide

vuosi year

vuotaa verta bleed

vyö belt

W

Wales Wales

WC restroom

WC toilet [BE]

WC-paperi toilet paper

Y

yhden hengen huone single room

yhdistää connect v

Yhdysvallat United States

yhtään any

yhteys connection (transportation, internet)

yksityinen private

yläkerta upstairs

yleensä usually

yleinen common (frequent)

yleinen general

yleislääkäri general practitioner [BE]

yliopisto university

ylitys crossing (maritime)

yllä, yli, yläpuolella above

ylös, ylhäällä up

ymmärtää understand

ympäri around the corner

yö night

yökerho dance club

yöpyä; jäädä; asua stay (trip); v (remain); v (reside)

yskä cough n

ystävä friend

ystävällinen; laatu kind adj; n

INDEX

Berlitz pocket guide

HELSINKI

Second Edition 2018

Editor: Carine Tracanelli
Author: Fran Parnell
Head of Production: Rebeka Davies
Picture Editor: Tom Smyth
Cartography Update: Carte
Update Production: Apa Digital
Photography Credits: Ari Karttunen/
EMMA 73; Bigstock 42; Getty Images 1, 15,
21, 30; Governing Body of Suomenlinna/
Dorit Salutskij 66; Gregory Wrona/Apa
Publications 6L, 34, 37, 92, 101, 104; Helsinki
Tourism 12, 24, 28, 84, 87; Helsinki Zoo/
Mari Lehmonen 70; iStock 4TC, 4MC, 4TL,
5TC, 5MC, 5M, 7L, 22, 26, 32, 83; Library
of Congress 18; Marketta Stenroth/Visit
Helsinki 65; Micah Sarut/Apa Publications
79, 80, 82; Public domain 5MC, 16;
Shutterstock 4ML, 5T; Visit Finalnd 74, 76,
77; Visit Helsinki 5M, 6R, 7R, 36, 39, 41, 44,
46, 49, 51, 52, 54, 56, 59, 61, 62, 68, 89, 91,
95, 97, 98, 107; VisitFinalnd/Juho Kuva 11;
VisitFinland 103
Cover Picture: iStock

Distribution

UK, Ireland and Europe: Apa Publications
(UK) Ltd; sales@insightguides.com
United States and Canada: Ingram
Publisher Services; ips@ingramcontent.com
Australia and New Zealand: Woodslane;
info@woodslane.com.au
Southeast Asia: Apa Publications (SN) Pte;
singaporeoffice@insightguides.com

Worldwide: Apa Publications (UK) Ltd;
sales@insightguides.com

**Special Sales, Content Licensing
and CoPublishing**
Insight Guides can be purchased in bulk
quantities at discounted prices. We can
create special editions, personalised jackets
and corporate imprints tailored to your
needs. sales@insightguides.com;
www.insightguides.biz

Contact us
Every effort has been made to provide
accurate information in this publication,
but changes are inevitable. The publisher
cannot be responsible for any resulting loss,
inconvenience or injury. We would appreciate
it if readers would call our attention to any
errors or outdated information. We also
welcome your suggestions; please contact
us at: berlitz@apaguide.co.uk
www.insightguides.com/berlitz